KINGDOM WRITERS
DEVOTIONAL
"Pulling On Heaven, Writing On Earth"

By

BRAE WYCKOFF

www.KingdomWritersAssociation.com

Copyright 2019 Brae Wyckoff
Kingdom Writers Devotional
KWA Publishing
©2019
Printed in USA

ISBN: 978-0-9997890-2-5
Library of Congress Control Number: 2019917554

Editor: Tiffany Vakilian
tiffany@tiffanyvakilian.com

Cover art by Sharon Marta of Marta Studios
http://www.martastudios.com

KINGDOM WRITERS
DEVOTIONAL
"Pulling On Heaven, Writing On Earth"

Contents

PROFESSIONAL INDUSTRY ENDORSEMENTS

"Passion-filled and Spirit-led, Kingdom Writers Association helps its members use their creative gifts to serve and honor the One who gave them."

Lynn Vincent- #1 *New York Times* bestselling writer of *Heaven is for Real* and *Same Kind of Different as Me*

Every pen, pencil, typewriter, or computer has the capacity to write a masterpiece.

However, it need not be a masterpiece to be meaningful!

When you show your faith, you can change a heart.

For me, Brae and Jill Wyckoff are the embodiment of God's word in 1 John 4:16, "God is Love."

Brae has progressed from non-believer to become a literary disciple for God.

As he expresses his goal to encourage writers of all ages to tell their stories, he is doing the work for his Heavenly Father, for God uses the written word as a pulpit.

**Peter Berkos
Academy Award Winner and Author**

Stories can be powerful and wonderful works of imagination and truth. However, one must answer a very basic question. Can I write a compelling and interesting story? The answer is a simple yes, but when you do, there are lessons to learn. There is joy in writing, but there are also rules and steps to successful writing. For the past 2 years, I have had the joy of attending the monthly Kingdom Writer's Association gatherings and have experienced Brae Wyckoff's leadership and encouragement. He is a masterful, accomplished storyteller and gifted teacher. The *Kingdom Writer's Devotional* is a precise guide and a gift to writers of all levels. You have the method of getting in touch with God, the Master Creator! The One who called you to write. Step by step, Brae gives you the tools you need to achieve what The Lord has planned for your work. Remember, it is really God's work *through* you. So, partner up with Him and use Brae's inspired book to teach you how.

Lawrence A Wood MD. Writers Guild
Author of crime series, *Among Pigeons*

"If you feel called to write, Brae's devotional will give you the inspiration and encouragement to write the story God has inside of you. If you are a writer, you will want to read the Kingdom Writer's Devotional."

Scott Evans
President & CEO of Outreach Inc.

Brae isn't just a competent writer that can weave together entertaining and meaningful content, he has the heart to equip others to do the same. This desire to assist a generation to create and release materials will change lives and affect the world. I cannot think of a more qualified and experienced person than Brae to take on this task. This book will inspire, prod, and give you the boost of confidence you need to take that next step of getting your material out for the world to read.

Brian Orme
Author of The Ascended Life
www.iborme.com

Brae awakens and equips modern-day scribes with both encouragement and coaching to fulfill their dreams. Like a good friend who comes alongside to bring wisdom to your journey, you'll find this book to be a powerful companion and Brae a steady source of encouragement in your writing process.

Rebecca Friedlander
Film Producer, Speaker, and Author of *Finding Beautiful:*
Discovering Authentic Beauty Around the World

Brae Wyckoff is a master storyteller as evidenced by his best selling Horn King series and his Historical Fiction novel, Demons & Thieves. In his new work, the Kingdom Writers Devotional, he unlocks the writing process and leads the reader into a deeper understanding of their personal writing assignment. This practical devotional will help the aspiring writer to build on their own ideas and get them to the finish line!

Bob Hasson
Author of *The Business of Honor* **with Danny Silk**
CEO Hasson Inc.

"Reading Brae Wyckoff's Kingdom Writer's Devotional was like drinking a Big Gulp of encouragement. He writes from a place of conviction, passion, and delight for writing and creativity that you can't help but be caught up into that same space and desire. I found myself immediately inspired to write with easy daily steps that bring focus, purpose, and action to the telling of their story. As someone once said, "All you really ever own is your story." I believe with all my heart that Brae's devotional will help any aspiring writers to step into the honor and privilege of owning and writing theirs."

Heather Nunn
One Sound Founder
USA Director Sounds of the Nations

According to numerous surveys over the years, 80% of people interviewed would like to write. The number of those who have written is much lower than that percentage. The reasons are many I am sure: confidence deficit, fear of failure, insufficient motivation, commitment shortage, and a host of other reasons.

Brae Wyckoff is an exceptionally gifted writer, but for your sake, he has great passion and gifting in assisting emerging writers to identify and overcome their personal obstacles, and to find their place in the world of writing.

I have read lots of books on writing by my favorite authors, and they have inspired me and helped me in many ways. However, *Kingdom Writers Devotional* is unique in its structure and content. Unfortunately, we have lost the art of storytelling, but the awesome thing is that every page in this book is a sign of Brae's commitment to helping the reader resurrect that ancient gift.

Towards the end of his life and in his last letter to his daughter, Abraham Heschel wrote these words, "Words create worlds." That is the goal of every writer, to create a new world for the reader that will take them to places unknown, inspiring them to reach beyond the ordinary.

Kingdom Writers Devotional will do exactly that, teach you how to create a new world where the writer replaces common, predictable concepts and phrases with unexpected and interesting ones that will build a new world for the reader.

There is a storyteller in every one of you. Brae will help you find your way.

Don Milam
Author Consultant, Whitaker House Publishers
Author, *The Ancient Language of Eden*

Brae has come up with a brilliant idea - a highly innovative devotional designed specifically for kingdom writers. Practical and prophetic in equal measure. Ideal for new and experienced writers, Brae offers gems of authorial wisdom on every page. I wish I'd thought of it myself!

Dr. Mark Stibbe
Bestselling, award-winning author,
and CEO of www.thebooklab.co.uk

With a heart for Kingdom Scribes and a desire to pull down Heavenly books from the "Story Vault", Brae Wyckoff has created a beautiful devotional that is both practical and encouraging. "Gathering all the Kingdom Scribes together and giving them space to write" has been Brae's mandate since the very beginning and to awaken these scribes to fulfill their own special mandates from God.

I would highly recommend *Kingdom Writers Devotional* to anyone who is even remotely thinking about writing; whether it is a book, movie script, or play. It will absolutely change the trajectory of your life as you pursue your calling as a Kingdom Scribe!

Sherry Ward
Square Tree Publishing, CEO

"How many of us have felt within us that God has something important for us to say? We might even dream of putting it into a book one day. But then, like the sudden spike of an electric surge, it peters out and ebbs away into nothing. Well, how would you like to read a book from someone who knows how to change that script? How would you like to take your inspired thoughts and get sage input and the spiritual encouragement to actually become one of God's kingdom scribes, one of his voices to a hungry and hurting world? Brae Wyckoff, president of the Kingdom Writer's Association, has written just such a gem. The *Kingdom Writer's Devotional* will inspire you on how to take the "inspiration" coming directly from God's Spirit, out from your mind and heart and onto the page. His layout of short, easily digestible chapters, are spot-on for what you need to hear, work through, and overcome. I predict this resource will be the guide for birthing scores of kingdom dreams. We're talking about the kinds of works that God has ordained in advance for you and me to do—the kinds that he will use to bless and change this world!"

- **Gary Comer, Author of** *ReMission: Rethinking How Church Leaders Create Movement* **and** *Soul Whisperer: Why the Church Must Change the Way it views Evangelism.*

Ever had one of those thoughts or times when you said, "I wish I had known or had this information then, that I have now?" That's what I thought when I looked at this devotional/instructional book from Brae. I've written one book. It should have been easy to write by pulling from all of my writings before, but it was one of the hardest things I've ever done. This devotional could have helped me. I loved Brae's simplicity, yet thoughtful way of approaching the story to get down on paper exactly what he wishes to convey and how his ideas translate to the writer so they can follow a tried and true path. I felt like Brae hit over and over on such a key element: allow the Holy Spirit to flow through you. He *IS* the Spirit of truth. And, isn't that what every writer wants; to write honestly, and from the heart--especially one guided by God. Whether you're a beginner writer or seasoned veteran, I believe this book will benefit and empower your writing.

Bill Dew
Dewnamis Ministries, Inc

This long-awaited devotional for writers will explode in your heart! Brae Wyckoff's new book, *Kingdom Writers Devotional- "Pulling On Heaven, Writing On Earth"*, cleverly provokes the reader to go deep! I know Brae, and he has an incredible love for people and writing. He inspires and trains any writer, at any level, to immerse into those deeper chambers of creativity. A powerful momentum emerges, as you allow a firestorm of writing to be released through each activation and prayer. This is more than a how-to book, it's a powerful tool. It's loaded with life-changing encounters that will delicately unravel the words of your story!

Maria Sainz
Co-founder Red Seal Ministries, San Diego

In a world full of opinions, it is important to separate meaningful conversations from white noise. In this devotional Brae not only takes thoughts and ideas straight on, but he also creates space for a conversation to take place. This is what he is brilliant at, creating space for people to start conversations…with other people and with God. I trust as you read these devotionals, your heart will be provoked to open up a new conversation. And of course, with the new conversation will come a new adventure. Happy adventure hunting!

Pastor Craig Muster
Director of Awakening International
Training & Reformation Center

I love to write because I believe I have something to say and that my words, hopefully, inspired by The Holy Spirit, will benefit others in their Kingdom journey...so I work at it, consistently, and hope that I am making an impact. I am told that I do. Though I love to write, the craft is not easy, and there are times of discouragement and frustration... so I am delighted to see a book like *Kingdom Writers Devotional* to help inspire and encourage writers like me in their journey. This is a wonderful gift to the Christian writer.

Stan E. DeKoven, Ph.D., MFT
President, Vision International
Author of 51 books and booklets to date

Walking through the *Kingdom Writers Devotional* is like sitting in a swing on an early Spring morning with that one friend who understands you as a writer in ways you are unable to understand yourself. And then... that precious friend gives you the skeleton key to finally unlock the fountain of ink within your spirit. Thank you, Brae, for understanding our journey so well and giving us this encouraging tool to move forward.

Theresa Harvard Johnson
The Scribal Conservatory Arts & Worship Center
Voices of Christ Apostolic Prophetic School of the Scribe

ALL GLORY TO CHRIST JESUS, MY LORD!

How This Book Will Benefit You As A Kingdom Writer

THIS DEVOTIONAL COMES with a warning.

If you are feeling discouraged, depressed, isolated, confused, and not sure where to start in general, then prepare your heart to receive your breakthrough. Wherever I go to speak, others around me get freed up in these areas as writers. I know this because I hear it time after time after my events. I speak to you today with confidence in the Holy Spirit to be working through me and into you as you read through this devotional.

Inside these pages you won't find a reading program such as "Day 1- Day 2", but you will find what the Holy Spirit has imparted to me over the years as His Kingdom Writer. Some chapters will be a simple reflection of thought, while others will be a deep revelation of God's Word. I have a strong gift of encouragement, and throughout this book, you will receive that impartation through my words for I believe that encouragement is the elixir of life for all writers.

This book is meant to be enjoyed, like a good cup of coffee or tea in the morning. Don't rush through it but embrace each section, and pray before reading to have Papa God reveal to you what you need at that time. The Holy Spirit is THE best teacher.

At the end of each devotional, you will see the following: Prayer and Action.

Action items are meant to push you deeper to explore your writing or to fire up your imagination. Some of these devotional actions are meant to be applied multiple times, such as journaling or reading scripture.

Prayer is me praying for you specifically on whatever topic we just discussed, or it is a prayer for you to recite over yourself.

Remember, you get out of this book what you apply yourself to. Meaning, if you just read the words but don't take it upon yourself to reflect, ponder, meditate, pray into, listen, learn, and apply action items then you get what you contributed. For example, I can read the Bible just to read it and mark it off my to-do list. BUT when I slow down, and look at each word, ponder its meaning, search out understanding the depth of what is written, then something gets deposited inside of me. It literally gets into my bones. That is what we are after here, to have this encouragement seep deep into your bones so you can become the Kingdom Writer you were always destined to be.

Be blessed and enjoy the Kingdom Writers Devotional—"Pulling on Heaven, writing on Earth".

WHO THE HECK IS
BRAE WYCKOFF?

IN A WORLD full of notable figures, celebrities, and Christian giants, I would ask the same thing.

God has led me and continues to lead me on a great adventure for His glory. In 2016, God called me out to be one of the leaders of His scribal army. You could say I'm one of the 'Special Ops' for the Kingdom, flying under the radar. Stories have captivated my heart since the age of five when I watched Luke Skywalker looking off into the distance toward twin suns, longing for something more. Or when I read about the children who discovered their destiny as they wandered the world of Narnia and met Aslan for the first time.

I embarked on the journey of writing in tenth grade. My English teacher declared me the winner of her short story contest out of thirty other students. I couldn't believe it, nor could several others. I was a hippy-kid that played on the school soccer team. I had semi-decent grades in all my classes, except English, which I was failing. Mrs. Henry said, "Brae wins not because of the content but because of his story." The content she was referring to was a delicious horror story, full of grotesque descriptions. BUT she said I won because of my ability to tell a story. From that point on, my calling to write was awakened.

It is necessary to mention that I was an atheist before I discovered the depth of God's Word. I gave my life over to Jesus on March 5th, 2000. After receiving Him into my heart, I devoured the Bible in less than seven months. I soon discovered He wrote about *me*. Here is one of the things He said. **Psalm 14:1(NIV) The fool says in his heart, "There is no God."**

Yeah, it is crazy but very true. God knew me. He clearly wrote about me. I was that fool. And then he called me, and I answered. It's a beautiful testimony, but that is for another time. My point is this; God writes about all of us. We just need to see differently to notice. He teaches us all things, even before we know Him personally. **Psalm 71:17 (NIV) Since my youth, God, you have taught me, and to this day I declare your marvelous deeds.**

A few years back, I had a unique encounter with God when I read this scripture one night. **Psalm 84:10 (NIV) "Better is one day in your courts than a thousand elsewhere."**

I heard Him tell me to change it to read the following: "Better is one story from you than a thousand elsewhere."

Now, you can read this two ways. My story is more important than a thousand tales elsewhere, or His story is more important than a thousand tales elsewhere. I don't believe this is an *either/or* but a *yes/and*. It's both. We look to God's stories and say one story from Him is better than anything. But, when God looks at our stories, He says it is our story that is more important than anything else. He is a loving Father who cherishes His children, and our stories are on his bookshelf for all to see. He is proud of what we do for Him.

Do you realize that you are a story being told? Do you realize the value you carry, the authority you wield, and the adventure you release to others around you? What story are you telling?

INTRODUCTION

ONE OF THE most important aspects of a story is the editor. The editor helps to shape the final product. The editor helps you decide what to cut and what to add.

Spiritually speaking, we have two editors in the world vying for our 'business.' The question is, "Who are you allowing to edit your story?"

Many fall victim to the lies of satan (who I call 'Little s'). He is, after all, the great deceiver. Because of this, he is allowed editing rights in their lives. He is editing the lives of those that are lost as well as those who believe. It's true! You and I are constantly fending off the editing notes of satan. If you know better, then you can see clearly what he is up to, and avoid his shenanigans. But to do that, you need to actively keep your spiritual eyes open to the reality of the situation. Actively keeping your spiritual eyes open simply means staying in God's Word, for His Word is a lamp unto our feet (Psalm 119:105).

Romans 12:2 (NIV) "Do not conform to the pattern of this world, but be transformed by the renewing of your mind. Then you will be able to test and approve what God's will is—his good, pleasing, and perfect will."

Don't conform to the pattern of this world. Who is in control of this world? satan, aka Little s. Conforming to this world is allowing satan editing access to our lives. It says not to conform, but instead be transformed by freshening, reviving, restoring, your mind. How? Let's look at **Ecclesiastes 2:13 (NIV)** "I saw that wisdom is better than folly, just as light is better than darkness." I absolutely love the direct message version, which says, "It's better to be smart than stupid." How and where do we get wisdom?

Psalm 119:105 (NKJV) "Your word is a lamp to my feet And a light to my path."

It is God's living Word that guides us, protects us. It is the Holy Spirit living inside of us, training us in all things (John 14:26). Is he not the author and finisher of our faith (Hebrews 12:2)?

Through this Kingdom Writers Devotional let the Holy Spirit teach and guide you, not me. I am sharing my journey, and through my journey, God will nudge you. He will open the eyes of your heart and give you a new revelation. I am imparting what He has given me to help propel you into your next level as a writer. My prayer is that the 'writing David' inside of you is released to pick up a pen and slay the giants before you.

What story are we writing for the world?

What story is Jesus writing through you for the world to see?

Now is your time. You were born for this. Take a deep breath and let God open your heart a little wider for His storytelling skills to go deeper than you ever could have imagined. The writer you dream of being is already there. God deposited the scribal ordination within you before the foundations, and it is time to collaborate with the Holy Spirit.

*"We each have a **writing assignment**, and the pages of destiny loom before us. In our hand, we hold the pen of truth filled with the ink of the Holy Spirit."* - **Brae Wyckoff**

SECTION ONE
CALLED TO WRITE

CHAPTER 1
GOD'S HANDIWORK

Ephesians 2:10- "For we are God's handiwork, created in Christ Jesus to do good works, which God prepared in advance for us to do."

H AS GOD CALLED you to write?
I can't speak for everyone else, but I know that if I don't write the stories inside me, then I feel incomplete. I call this the *Scribe's calling.* There is a calling on us scribes that tugs at our heart to release what is inside of us. Why? Look at the verse above in Ephesians. We *are* God's handiwork. Wow! That alone is enough. But He continues! We were created in Christ Jesus to do good works. Double wow! But wait, there's more. God prepared in advance for us to do these good works. Are you kidding me? This is music to my heart and soul. God literally prepared us to do these things. Subconsciously, we tap into our calling, this preparedness, to do the things we were called to do. For a scribe it is or should be obvious, I've got to WRITE!

It is time to step into your destiny and let your voice be heard. You *are* God's handiwork and what God creates is not substandard. The enemy wants you to think that you're not enough, that you don't have what it takes. He wants you to compare yourselves to others to point out your flaws, BUT GOD! God is the final say, not the enemy lying to you. Your creator created you in Christ Jesus to do what? Good works! Not just any good works, but works specific to you and formed in you before the foundations.

I love the Passion Bible translation for this same verse:

We have become his poetry, a re-created people that will fulfill the destiny he has given each of us, for we are joined to Jesus, the Anointed One. Even before we were born, God planned in advance our destiny and the good works we would do to fulfill it.

It is so incredible to read verses like this. He thought of us. Let it seep into your bones. Imagine that God knew you before you were even conceived. He planned your destiny, AND the good works you would be doing to fulfill that very destiny.

Doesn't that inspire awe within you?

Now, Ephesians 2:10 requires action on our part. I am referring to the good works "we" would "do" to fulfill our calling. God did His part. Now we must do ours. For a child of The Most High, this is a great mantle, but for creatives (especially us scribes), this can mean so much more. Can you feel the stirring inside you to write? Verses like this are the spark needed to ignite the fueled destiny inside of you. You have a God-sized destiny waiting to come alive. Despite the world continuously pulling on you and me to go after a worldly destiny—a shallow one, without form, and hopeless. We simply say, "YES!" to what God has in store for each of us. We have to continue to show up and walk out our destiny. Sitting on the couch and saying, "God tell me what you want me to do," then wait while we watch TV or do something else mundane is not going to cut it. We need to actively pursue our calling. 'Little s' wants us to remain in a program where we repeat the same things everyday. It is time to change it up. Do something different. Do something that inspires you and be intentional on listening to what God has to say to you during that time. Inspiration is a door to breakthrough. Encouragement is the key.

Stay focused on the destiny that God designed for you specifically. It is built into your DNA. Pull-on heaven and write on earth.

My Prayer to the reader: Lord, I bless the reader in your mighty name. Let your words infiltrate deep into their heart to the point of breaking off any lies spoken over them that they are not good enough, that they don't matter. We give you permission to write on our heart your truth, Lord, that you designed us perfectly and planned in ADVANCE our destiny and the books we would write in your name. We love you, God, and praise your holy name.

Action: Read Ephesians 2:10 over yourself each day for the next 30 days. Memorize it. It can also help to write the verse down each day to help you remember it.

CHAPTER 2
I WILL SEND YOU SCRIBES

*Matthew 23:34 (ESV) Therefore I send you prophets
and wise men and scribes, some of whom you will kill
and crucify, and some you will flog in your synagogues
and persecute from town to town,*

IN ORDER TO combat all the evil that is being released into the world,
God is releasing prophets, wise men, and scribes.

I spoke on this scripture at the Kingdom Creativity Conference
in 2017. Matthew 23 is all about the Seven Woes to the Scribes and
Pharisees. Take a moment to read through Matthew 23:1-33. You can
read any (or all) of the versions, which is a good idea, but the Lord
actually instructed me to read the ESV for this particular teaching.

Now, how are you feeling by the end of verse 33? Encouraged?
Probably not. This is a harsh word from Jesus to the scribes and the
Pharisees. But read verse 34.

Here in this verse is a word that is found 526 other times in the
New Testament; "therefore." In the Greek, this word translates to 'oun'.
Oun is typically translated *"therefore,"* which means, *"By extension,*
here's how the dots connect." Verses 1 through 33 were brutal truths of
where the scribes were at. Jesus then says in verse 34, "Therefore." Or
"Here's how the dots connect, I send you prophets and wise men and
SCRIBES."

God is releasing the Shawn Bolz' into the world, He is releasing the
Ravi Zacharias' into the world, He is releasing the Kingdom Writers
(you) into the world!

Get excited! Do you see it? You are part of this verse. He wrote this with you and me in mind. It is time to pick up your weapon (pen) and fight (write). There are horrible books being released into the world daily. Some forums have suggested that 1,000 to 5,000 books are published on Amazon each day alone. It is our assignment to combat this evil with Kingdom revelation, with Kingdom stories. This is your time. This is your season. You were strategically placed where you are for a reason. Whatever the enemy of this world throws at you, whether it be a horrible act against you, a missing parent in your life, some kind of addiction, pain, suffering, whatever it is, God will and can redeem it. He sent you. Look at verse 34 again, but look at it personally. Replace the word "scribe" with your name. Personalize it. And once you do that, then own it. Write with holy passion, and do it with God.

Prayer: Thank you, God, for sending us. Thank you, God, for calling us as your scribes. I pray that each of us will rise up to the calling you have placed upon us and write with a holy passion to glorify your name. I pray for an army of Kingdom Scribes to rise up, write the award-winning books, reach more people for Christ, train others in your ways as a scribe, and bring a revival like we have never seen before. Let us be focused as your Kingdom Scribe to promote your name while at the same time you elevate us in man's eye. As Jesus increased in favor with man and God, let it be so with us as well.

Action: Write verse 34 in your journal. Then write out the same verse but instead personalize it by adding in your name.

CHAPTER 3
IMITATE ME

Ephesians 5:1 "Imitate God, therefore, in everything you do, because you are his dear children."

MOST OF US look at this verse and say, "Okay, imitate God in everything He does." I instantly think of healing the sick, casting out demons, raising the dead, right?

But what about writing?

There's a simple answer to that. I'll pose it in the form of a question.

Did God not write the Bible?

This is one of my favorite verses as a writer. I spoke about this verse at the 2018 Kingdom Creativity Conference in San Diego. In the Passion Translation, it says, "Be imitators."

This is a challenge toward us. Imitate God in EVERYTHING we do. God wrote the Book of all books. The Bible has been the number one bestseller since it was first printed. It sells (on average) 50 books per minute, with an estimated 6 billion copies sold (and counting). This verse is a God-sized challenge to us to imitate God as scribes. Did you know that it took God over 1500 years to write the Bible? He used 40 writers, spanning 40 generations, consisting of 20 occupations, written in 10 countries, covering over 6 thousand miles. Now, there may be 40 writers, BUT there is only 1 author.

He is the Author and Finisher of our faith.

He co-labored with us, His creation, to create His written word!

And His Word stands forever. Let's get back to the challenge. Do you like a good challenge? Well, here is the ultimate one...Imitate God!

That's right, write the best book you can possibly create, but do it with God, not by yourself. You see, God co-labored with us to write His book. Why would we not do the same? What possible reason would there be to leave Him out? We are to imitate Him in EVERYTHING we do. So we write our books or whatever writing assignment with Him.

This world groans for the next story (good, bad, or ugly). We are a story-eating machine, always longing for the next tale to be told. Your story could be one of the good ones, or one of the God ones, pulled directly from heaven itself. It takes an open heart ready to receive and hard work. Yes, *hard* work.

REMEMBER, YOUR STORY COULD TAKE SOME TIME TO DEVELOP.

God wants us to increase our skills, to continue to develop our writing, and get the proper training. You might publish a book or two before he deems you ready for a Kingdom story waiting in heaven for a Storyteller Champion to take it on. Don't give up. Stay true to your calling. If he has called you, then let nothing stand in your way (especially what the enemy throws at you). He is your King. He is your God. Your eyes are focused on Him. Give Him room to speak.

Prayer Challenge: Pray this prayer if you think you are ready. It will prepare you in thinking on heavenly things as we are instructed to do.

Lord, bless me with YOUR story. I want to write what no ear has heard or eye has seen in this world. Send me the story you want me to write with you. Let it glorify your name and not mine. I pray you would open the "Story Vault" in heaven and send it to me. I'm your willing scribe. Let my pen become a mighty weapon to bring what is unseen to the seen. I humbly ask this in Jesus' name.

Action: Pray the above and then close your eyes. Concentrate as you imagine yourself inside the "Story Vault" in heaven. As images come to your mind, write them down in your journal. Brainstorm with God. Some of what you write down might be the title of a story. It might be a scripture He leads you to read where new revelation will be given to you. Whatever you see, write it down. We first need the seed of a story, and God wants to plant those stories inside of us.

CHAPTER 4
IT TAKES PASSION

1 Corinthians 9:24 "Do you not know that in a race all the runners run, but only one gets the prize? Run in such a way as to get the prize."

WRITING A BOOK doesn't happen on its own--it takes perseverance, discipline, and a passion for completing it.

Think of it as losing weight. It requires us to go to the gym and put the effort in, consistently, not just once or twice, but making a lifestyle change to lose weight and keep it off. The same is true for writing a book. We need to sit in a chair and write consistently each day until it becomes a lifestyle.

In this scripture, it shows us that there are many runners, but only ONE gets the prize. Are you the one to give up the prize because it's just too hard? Or, are you willing to take each step, one at a time, until you are running the race? Not just any race but *your* race. This is your life. This is your time.

The last part of the scripture says to run in such a way as to get the prize. To get the prize, we need to position ourselves. Positioning requires our 'game-face'. It requires an emotional stance, a determination, a desire that transcends all other desires. When we have a book that needs to be written, it won't write itself. We need to run in such a way that lines up with the calling we have as scribes and cross the finish line.

There is another facet to the last part of this scripture. It implies running "your" race. Not just any race but running in such a way that represents you. Each of us is unique. There is no one in the world like you, not now or anytime in the past or in the future. God strategically placed you in this time, in this place, in the family you are part of, in the world you live in, and so on.

Let's replace the word run with the word 'write'.

Write in such a way as to get the prize.

If we all wrote about the same subject and even gave the same starting sentence, we would all come back with something different. We would not write the same. Do you get it? Do you understand the true power of who you are as a writer? God has called you to write. It is time to answer His call and write in such a way as to get the prize.

If we don't speak, then our voice won't be heard. If we don't write, then the world misses out on hearing about God in our unique identity in Christ. This isn't about you and at the same time it is about you. It's about us showing up and fulfilling our assignment, our Kingdom Writers assignment.

Prayer: Lord, God Almighty, we praise you and thank you for our unique voice as writers. We want to co-labor with you to write and represent your Kingdom. Thank you for sending us. Thank you for calling us as your scribe. Bless the words that we string together to form a sentence. Bless the sentences we string together that form a story. Bless our minds as we create worlds with our words in Jesus' name.

Action: Write one sentence each day this week. Don't miss a single day. At the end of seven days, you will have a paragraph. On week two, write two sentences each day. One sentence a day is like putting on your running shoes. You are preparing your mind for the race ahead. As runners, we need to prepare. Writing two sentences a day is like stretching after you put your shoes on. You are letting your body know to get ready. It is time to run.

CHAPTER 5
GOD CHOSE YOU

John 15:16 (TPT) "You didn't choose me, but I've chosen and commissioned you to go into the world to bear fruit. And your fruit will last, because whatever you ask of my Father, for my sake, he will give it to you!"

GOD CHOSE YOU and authorized you to go into the world and yield positive results with your writing.

Let's look at the word 'commissioned'. Here is the definition: *[to] give an order for or authorize the production of (something such as a building, piece of equipment, or work of art).*

Sit back and think about that. Wow! That is quite a commissioning from God. Do you realize that He chose us for this assignment? We were chosen. You were chosen.

Look at the next part of the verse, "fruit that will last." Your story will last. It will endure. It will be passed down from generation to generation. This phrase goes even deeper than that. It speaks of the essence of what you will release. You have the authority to ask the Father to give you the power to change lives when they read your work. You can have a supernatural impartation released through your words. You could touch that one reader who will change the world in the best ways because they read *your* work. That is crazy awesome.

Imagine it. A young adult coming to you with tears in their eyes, talking about your book. This has happened to me numerous times with my stories, and it never gets old. They come to me to talk about a specific scene that deeply touched them. During their explanation, the tears fall freely. What is it that caused that encounter or those tears? It's not just a good sentence or story. There is an impartation we receive from God to write. He commissioned us. He gave us authority. We 'pull on Heaven and write on Earth,' which is powerful and lasting. That is why those readers who encounter our Kingdom Writings are moved in such a powerful way.

Think beyond the here and now. Think about a time after you are gone, and one person is led by the Holy Spirit to read your work. Perhaps they are about to commit suicide, but God directs them to this dust-covered book in some thrift store. They read it. God transforms their life by reading it. They accept Christ into their heart. They find their identity as a citizen of Heaven. They end up fulfilling their assignment and become the next Billy Graham.

Don't discount what God will do with your writings. Be obedient and answer the call you have on your life.

Prayer: Lord, thank you for commissioning us. Thank you for calling our names. Thank you for choosing us as your Kingdom scribe. I pray that we will represent you well. I pray that our stories will impact the hearts of the most hardened men and women in the world. I pray that our words will supernaturally set people free, bind up the wounded, cast out demons, and ultimately open up hearts to your invading love.

Action: Write in your journal the scripture above and then write what you feel this verse is speaking to you personally. God chose you. Why? God commissioned to bear fruit. What does that look like to you? Fruit that will last. What are you planting? What kind of fruit do you want to bear?

CHAPTER 6
WAKE UP!

Revelation 3:2 (TPT) "Wake up and strengthen all that remains before it dies, for I haven't found your works to be perfect in the sight of my God."

OUR WRITING MUST be as excellent as possible to bring before the throne of God.

Is this not a call to arms? Wake up! Strengthen ALL that remains before it goes away! Lay your work before Him and have Him burn away the impurities within its pages.

For believers to be in mainstream marketing, we need to wake up and truly strengthen our work. I'm not saying compromise, I'm saying we need to write the stories that God wants us to write, and do so with excellence.

I've seen writers come to the end of their projects and think, "Ahh, perfection!" But despite their diligence and dedication, they were deeply humbled when their work was rejected, received bad reviews, or their sales were dismal. Find people who will critique your work before it goes to print, and be open to the possibility of extensive editing. I'm not talking about having your mom read your work but people that will give you a good solid critique about your book. Sorry, mom, but you love us so well it is hard for you to tell us the truth that we need to hear. Every person has an opinion and what you need to hear are those opinions. Get friends that you trust and even people you don't know that well and ask them to give you feedback. You can't please everyone but what you are looking for are comments that revolve around the same area of the story or a common thread. Those are the areas that you will need to take a hard look at and develop it further.

Hone the story to become a masterpiece. You can't be a Kingdom Scribe and treat your work as a hobby. Make your time for writing just as important as getting up to your alarm clock and going off to work each day.

HONE THE STORY TO BECOME A MASTERPIECE.

Yes, God gave you the story, I understand, BUT now it's important to steward it wisely—advance it with excellence. Of course, God will be with you, but don't assume that what you wrote is perfect as is. A good author asks multiple beta readers to give solid, honest feedback. Once beta reader comments are taken into account, the final step is to HIRE a professional editor. Don't skip this last part. It's imperative that we produce quality work—work that will rise above what is currently on the market.

Prayer: Thank you, God. Thank you for pushing us to be excellent writers. Thank you for showing us how to do that by writing the book of all books. I pray that we follow you and dedicate ourselves to write for your Kingdom. Let our writings be a blessing to you, and we give you permission right now to correct us, to guide us, and to show us where we need to make changes. We write because we love you. We write because you gifted us to be your scribe. Thank you for calling us and thank you for believing in us.

Action: Write a short story no longer than three pages and then have someone read it and give you feedback. Take the feedback and rewrite the story using their suggestions as you see fit. You don't have to make changes to everything they say, but look it over and really ponder the comments made.

The story could be about anything. Here is a suggested writing prompt: "You are Apostle Peter in a boat on the Sea of Galilee. There is a violent storm, and through the rain, you see what appears to be a ghost coming closer to you and your friends. Write a story describing what you see, feel, and hear. Write your story from Peter's point of view. Write from his perspective."

If you have already written something, such as your project, then print out one to three chapters and have a few people look it over and give their feedback to you.

CHAPTER 7
ONE BOOK OR TWO?

2 Peter 3:1 (NASB) This is now, beloved, the second letter I am writing to you in which I am stirring up your sincere mind by way of reminder,

YOU MIGHT THINK that you only have one book in you. You might think that the story of your life is all there is. You might think that you will only write in one genre, like me. This book will actually be my 7th published book and will become my 4th genre. I started writing epic fantasy and believed that was all that I would ever write. Then I wrote a children's book, a historical fiction, and now non-fiction.

Is it not true that we need to be reminded of things, not once but many times? Is it not true that we need to hear the same sermon through multiple voices and multiple perspectives to get it into our bones? I love it when writers come to me and say they just have one book in them. I smile and encourage them to get that one book out! But I know they are called for more. We can write that one book, but the calling inside won't go away. Our calling propels us into a world of wonder, but a neglected calling becomes a haunting weight upon us. When you exercise your destiny, it brings you life. So it is with being a Kingdom Writer.

It's okay to focus solely on the one without getting caught up on what is next. In fact, you should not be focusing on the next if you have not yet released your first. Get that first book out.

For those of you who have published your first book and thought that was it, that you were done, I challenge you to read this scripture again, pray into it, and hear what the Holy Spirit says.

Once a scribe, always a scribe.

Prayer: Thank you for the many chapters of our own lives. I pray that the chapters you have written in our hearts transcribe into multiple books. Shower us with Kingdom stories. Challenge us to write and produce works for generations to come. You called us to be your scribe. Let us heed that calling. Let us rise up to the challenge and the bear the fruit in your glorious name. It is a privilege to write for you and with you. Like the air we breathe, let us bring life to others with the words that flow from us onto the page. We declare this in Jesus' name.

Action: Write a letter to yourself. In this letter, indicate your goals as a Kingdom scribe. List out the book you are writing and the purpose of that book. Then write about another book that you have not yet thought about. It could just be an idea, or it could be just telling yourself that you want to write another book after this, but you don't know what it is.

Now, seal up the letter in an envelope. On the outside of the envelope, tell yourself to open this in one to three years (place the date one to three years later on when you wrote it). Then tuck it away in a safe place. When those years pass, you will be amazed at what God has done with your willing heart. He will answer prayers you hadn't even prayed yet.

CHAPTER 8
LET'S GO TO THE OTHER SIDE

Mark 4:35 (NIV) That day when evening came, he said to his disciples, "Let us go over to the other side."

As a writer called to write, I ask you this question, "What is in your way?"

This is a fantastic verse for us as writers and for us as believers in general.

What are you talking about Brae? How does this apply to my writing?

Well, let's break it down a bit. This is when Jesus and His disciples are about to face a huge storm, the kind that had even experienced fishermen fearing for their lives. What was Jesus doing? He was resting. No, not just resting but sleeping. He was sleeping so soundly that the disciples had to wake Him up. We ask this question all the time, "Why was Jesus sleeping?" We could just settle on the fact that He is God and it doesn't matter, but that's not a correct way of thinking. Jesus did everything on purpose.

Look at what He said again, "Let us go over to the other side." It wasn't just a comment. Jesus didn't just think or say, "Hey, I'm bored so let's jump in this boat and see what's over there." No, Jesus was making a statement. A declaration. He was repeating what the Father told Him. Go to the other side. Jesus was sleeping because He knew that nothing could prevent Him from getting to the other side.

I wrote this specific scene out in my historical fiction novel, *Demons & Thieves.* The two demon-possessed men on the Gerasene shore (on the other side by the way) knew Jesus was coming. They brought the storm down upon the men in the boat, hoping to prevent Jesus and the disciples from reaching their side. Well, Jesus calms the storm and looks at His disciples and asks them what? "Do you still have no faith?"

It begs the question - What is faith?

Hebrews 11:1 says, "Now faith is confidence in what we hope for and assurance about what we do not see."

Each man in the boat heard Jesus say, "Let us go over to the other side." The storm distracted them from this truth. The storm brought fear to them, and the fear took over. Our faith is not in the seen but in the unseen. Faith is confidence and assurance in what we hope for that we do not see. Jesus said they were going to the other side. There was no stopping that.

What happened when they got to the other side? They immediately encountered the demon named Legion. Consider this; the demon named Legion was never Jesus' mission. The mission was always the demon-possessed men and Legion was in HIS way. That is powerful. It wasn't by chance they were there. Jesus was sent on a mission. He cast out the demon and then continued on His mission.

Are you letting the storms of life bring fear and doubt into your writing? Are you focusing on your situation instead of the promise? God said to you, "Come on, let's go to the other side." As a Kingdom Writer called to write, God is saying, "Come on, let's write that book." And if He is saying that, then I ask you this question once again, "What is in your way?"

Prayer: Lord, bless our minds, our hearts, and our bodies as we take on the waves of life. Help us keep our focus on you and not the distractions. You have declared us worthy even if we haven't. Help us to see things from your perspective. Help us see the other side. I pray that our words will be bold and beautiful and reach thousands of people. Bless our writings, bless our scribal journey, our scribal adventures. Let us find peace in the pocket of writing. Bring clarity to our thoughts, and we pray that we glorify your name above anything else we do. Amen!

Action: Memorize Hebrews 11:1 and repeat daily before writing. Then follow it up by saying, "It is time to go to the other side."

CHAPTER 9
SILENCED BY REJECTION

1 Peter 2:4 (NIV) "As you come to him, the living Stone—rejected by humans but chosen by God and precious to him—"

HOW MANY VOICES have been silenced by rejection? Too many to count.

Rejection is huge with all of us.

It can devastate us so much so that it incapacitates us from our true calling. I had to overcome feelings of rejection before I began to truly walk in my calling. Over the years, God has shown me my true voice as a writer. It came from Him, but it was shaped, held up, held back, and ultimately released by my choice to partner with Him. Once I did, He opened up opportunities to help others step into their calling; to equip, empower, and encourage them in their walk with God as a Kingdom Writer. You are a Kingdom Writer. Identity is everything.

Even our Lord and Savior had to deal with identity. Jesus received his identity just before He was baptized. God said, "This is my son, in whom I am well pleased." Why did Jesus need to hear this? Didn't He already know who He was?

The answer, of course, is yes, but remember, Jesus is God in bodily form—He's human. Hearing that heavenly word galvanized Him to go forward. That word was a shield against the rejection He would ultimately feel, and believe me, he *felt* it--figuratively and literally. Look at us. We have people around us who love us, but we still need to hear it, don't we?

Now, immediately after he was baptized, what happened? Jesus was driven into the wilderness, where He was tempted by Satan. Satan is the ultimate deceiver, perverting scripture to make us think differently but it is our identity in who God says we are that shines a bright light onto the darkest of lies. Satan tried Jesus, hoping to thwart his destiny. Papa God said, "I love you son. Nothing will change that. Don't forget it." And that was all Jesus needed to get Him through the trials. That is all we need to get us through our trials. Knowing who we are. We are His! We are not rejected. We are beloved! No matter what, Jesus loves us, He died for us, and He set us free from the lies of this world.

Now, Kingdom Scribe, God has called you to write. And if He called you, then He is with you. He is for you. You cannot fail. Write from that foundation--with Him, and knowing who you are. Don't worry about writing perfectly, just write.

I have written so many things that were not of God, but I wrote anyway. I may not have done it perfectly, but I did it knowing who I was. Later, when we went through the editing process, things got refined by the fire. Don't worry about the content of what you are writing, just write. Get it out!

And do it knowing who and whose you are in Christ Jesus.

Once you have it out, then the Holy Spirit, along with you, will co-labor together and eliminate things that were of the flesh. Enjoy the process *with* God. Work *with* Him. Remember, He is for you.

Pray this prayer: "I am a son of God. I am loved by God. I may be rejected by humans, but I am never rejected by you. I know who I am and I know that God loves me no matter what. Let me write as a son/daughter of God. Let me keep in step with the Spirit of God and write Kingdom truths. Let me have ears to hear you, God. Let me have eyes to see you, God. Let me be fully alive and walking into the destiny you have called me into."

Action: Go to a mirror where it is private. Probably in your bathroom. Now, stare at yourself. Look yourself in the eyes. Study yourself. Look beyond the physical and start whispering to yourself that you are a son/daughter of God. Tell yourself that you cannot fail. Tell yourself that your voice matters. Tell yourself that your words matter. Repeat this daily until it sinks in.

This is a strange action item but what you are doing is speaking life into your very soul. You are speaking to your identity and pushing past any emotions that try to block who you are. Our emotions can be fickle, but our identity is secure in Christ. It is time to anchor yourself in that truth. Your writing will be upgraded when you start believing in who you are and what God wants to do in and through you as His Kingdom Writer.

SECTION TWO
PLUNDER THE DARKNESS

PLUNDER THE DARKNESS

"WRITE WHAT YOU know and then make up the rest," is my motto as a fiction writer.

The question is, "What do you know?"

As a writer, you will always put a little bit about yourself into those labored pages. The reader might never know, but you do.

So what does, "Plunder the darkness" really mean?

I'm talking about all the things that the enemy has done to you. All the lies. All the pain. All the illnesses. All the hurts. All the betrayals. All the death and destruction. *Everything.* This is the darkness that tries to wage war inside of us. The darkness we wrestle with. The darkness that contends for our time. We can (we must) plunder it! It is time to loot, pillage, rob, raid, ransack, strip, fleece, ravage, lay waste, devastate, maraud, sack, everything the enemy has stolen from us. We don't hold back.

We can only plunder this darkness when we understand who we are in Christ and whose we are in God. Jesus set us free on the cross, right? Yes. Papa God gave us the right to be called children of God, correct? Yes! We are now free. We are now a son/daughter to the King of kings. This is a powerful change to life as we have known it! We are no longer an orphan but adopted forevermore into the Kingdom of Heaven. We are citizens of Heaven. Furthermore, we are now Ambassadors, representatives, of God. Let that sink in!

Are you with me? Are you tracking with me? Why not use our life testimony to strengthen the stewarding of our representation of the Most High? As a believer in Christ Jesus, you are a new creation. Our old self is no longer in control. As a person saved by the blood of Christ, I can now look into this darkness, this past of mine, and go into it without fear because I know who I am. I am a son of God.

I can now plunder the enemy and take back everything he stole and more!

Let me give you an example of what I'm talking about in this section of the book. This is an important part of your walk as a Kingdom Scribe. You must be able to plunder your own darkness.

All of us have had bad things happen to us, whether it be molestation, rape, deep wounds by family and friends, divorce, separated children, violence in the home or in war, and the list goes on. Now, I firmly believe that as a believer in Christ Jesus, we can go into these dark places and pull out the emotions, the hurts, the pains, and place it within a story we are weaving with God and write, bringing healing breakthrough. This healing might not have happened for you directly, but once you became a believer in Christ you became a NEW creation. The old has passed. We can tap into the memories and pull on them into our writings. When others read our stories there is a supernatural impartation that occurs to the reader. Much like what happens when we read the Bible and allow the words to penetrate our heart.

As you read the next several chapters, "Plunder the Darkness" will expand your understanding. Remember, the Holy Spirit is the best teacher so let Him speak to you as you read these chapters.

CHAPTER 10
GO BACK INTO THE DARKNESS

Exodus 3:21-22 (AMP) And I will grant this people favor and respect in the sight of the Egyptians; therefore, it shall be that when you go, you will not go empty-handed. But every woman shall [insistently] ask her neighbor and any woman who lives in her house, for articles of silver and articles of gold, and clothing; and you shall put them on your sons and daughters. In this way you are to plunder the Egyptians [leaving bondage with great possessions that are rightfully yours]."

W HAT THE ENEMY took from me is now a mighty weapon in the hands of a Kingdom Writer.

God instructs Moses to have the Israelites go back and plunder the Egyptians of all that was taken from them. The Israelites had a slave mindset. They didn't think to take anything more than their meager belongings, but God wanted them freed from a slave mentality. They were to plunder and bring with them not just their meager belongings but also what belonged to their enemies. This applies to each of us as believers. We were once lost, and now we are found. We were once blind, but now we can see. We were once orphans but now grafted into the vine with God. Those who believe are now children of God. We are no longer slaves but now a family. Our inheritance was once hell, and now it is eternal life. Do you see? God wants us to take dominion of our lives just like when he wanted Adam and Eve to take dominion over the world and everything in it. Anything that was robbed of our youth, our innocence, God wants us to plunder and take back interest from what was stolen. He not only freed us but now he wants us to go back and take possession of the gold and silver. Our darkest times has gold and silver within it. Don't be afraid to go there because you are not alone. God is with you. Don't delve the depths of darkness without Him.

In the same way, spiritually, we, as writers, will be able to go back into the darkness (as free people) and take out what we need. It is not only available to us, but it is also part of our individual arsenal in this war for the Kingdom.

For example, my childhood was not your typical childhood. At the age of five, I was introduced to pornography and drugs. It was all around me until I married at the age of twenty-one. I grew up way too fast. In some ways, you would say my childhood was stolen from me. Well, today, as a firm believer in Jesus Christ and pursuing Him with everything I've got, I ended up writing two children's books. I plundered an area that was stolen from me. Now my children's books reach people around the world--not just children! Adults are influenced as they read my books out loud to their kids. It is an incredible blessing.

I can go into the darkest places in my past, pull whatever I need into the light and express it through writing.

I don't have to write an autobiography about my life. I can take my experiences and weave the truth into my storytelling, mostly in fictional novels. Every book you read has this element within its pages. Every character is a piece of the author, but what piece only the author knows.

As Kingdom representatives, we can impart powerful Kingdom truths to those that read our works within our writings, whether they are believers or not.

We have the opportunity to affect people with our words. This is not a small calling!

I have had grown men talk to me about my epic fantasy series and break down in tears. One time, a man expressed to me that he deeply connected with the vampire and the internal conflict he struggled with. It had a lasting impact on him. This particular part of my book, The Vampire King, was born from my own pains, my own darkness. I plundered those places and released into my story, characters covered in the blood of the Lamb. The result was a supernatural impartation.

It's imperative that you get yourself healthy and whole in Jesus. It is the first step you must take before you start plundering. The enemy is still roaming and always in the business of lies and deceit, pain, and destruction. Once you come to terms with the fact that you are a son of God, you will be ready to plunder the darkness. Your identity must be secure in this knowledge first. Let the Holy Spirit guide you.

God will show you the way, and sometimes you won't even realize you were plundering the darkness all along. God showed me what happened after I wrote my children's books. I didn't write them with the mindset of plundering. He revealed this to me a year later. God is all about redeeming you, so we focus on staying in step with Him. Signs and wonders will follow.

Pray this prayer: "Holy Spirit, guide me in my writing. Help me navigate the darkness to take all that I need and more to bring you Glory. Let me feast heartily before my enemies as I write in the joy of the Lord. You are my everything and nothing in this world has power over me because I am forever yours. Let my writings impact everyone who reads them to give you opportunities to penetrate their heart with the truth, love, and power of Christ Jesus our Lord."

| **Action:** Write in your journal. "I am a son of God. Period." |

CHAPTER 11
STORY AWAY!

Ephesians 5:11-14 (TPT) And don't even associate with the servants of darkness because they have no fruit in them; instead, reveal truth to them. The very things they do in secret are too vile and filthy to even mention. Whatever the revelation-light exposes, it will also correct, and everything that reveals truth is light to the soul. This is why the Scripture says, "Arise, you sleeper! Rise up from the dead and the Anointed One will shine his light into you!"

A WRITER HAS THE unique ability, gifting from God, to bring revelatory truth through stories.

There are many Bible verses that jump out at me as a writer. This one says to not associate or engage with those who walk in darkness but instead reveal the truth to them. How do we do this? Through stories. All of humanity longs for the next tale. Imagine your book going to the darkest places and bringing Kingdom light and truth to the one reading it. You are now considered "special ops" for the Kingdom. You can get to places no one else can. A pedophile, a murderer, a thief, a prostitute, an evil king, a terrorist, and the list goes on. A story is literally a battering ram into someone's heart. Once their barrier splinters, even a fraction, that's when the Holy Spirit dives in.

I love Star Wars. It makes such great symbols for me to use! Imagine everyone's heart is the Death Star, an impenetrable fortress. You are a pilot within a small X-Wing fighter. Your mission is to take on a heavily armed battle station. And the only way to destroy it is to release proton torpedoes into a small reaction chamber that leads to the core. I call these 'story bombs'. As you release your book into the world you yell out, "Story away!"

Our stories will penetrate the darkest hearts. As black as pitch, the light never seen, a person's heart can be opened with a story. Jesus did just that wherever He went. He never spoke to a crowd without telling them a parable. God continues to speak to our hearts through story-telling. Movies, books, music, poetry. God is not silent.

There is so much noise in the world we live in. This day to day noise vies for our attention, whether we are asleep or awake. Take notice of what happens when you personally engage with a movie and are engrossed in the story. It can supernaturally penetrate your heart and change your belief system. You can literally walk out of a theater and be changed. The same is true with a book. Stories shift mindsets. Stories shift hearts. Stories shift cultures.

Don't underestimate the power of the HOLY FORCE! Remember, anything is possible with God. Your stories matter.

The world we live in is being bombed by worldly stories. It is time we fight back like the Rebels against the Empire in the Star Wars saga. It is time we bring Kingdom stories to life.

Prayer: "Jesus, thank you for showing us how to tell stories. Thank you for revealing to us the importance that Father God places on storytelling for you didn't do anything or say anything without the Father telling you. Let it be so with our writing. Let us have ears to hear you, God. We want the stories you want told to be released into the world. Take our stories into the darkest of dark and explode into brilliant victorious light and reach the hearts no one thought possible. All glory of your power, might, and love be to you. Bless our writing in Jesus' name."

Action: Watch Star Wars IV: A New Hope—specifically the battle scene against the Death Star. Imagine you being Luke Skywalker and releasing your story into the death star hearts of people. Your story will cause a chain reaction explosion inside and prepare their hearts to receive God's truth.

Youtube search 'Luke destroys the Death Star'.

CHAPTER 12
STORYTELLER CHAMPION

1 Samuel 10:25(NKJV) Then Samuel explained to the people the behavior of royalty, and wrote it in a book and laid it up before the Lord.

LAY YOUR WORK before Him, for without His blessing, what are our works worth?

Have you ever heard someone speak that really moved you? Afterward, you need to hear it again, or you are running to the book table to grab your copy to pour into the next chance you get. Samuel explained to everyone the behavior of royalty, its power, authority, and greatness. This was before books were printed. The people wanted and needed to hear it again, so Samuel wrote it all in a book. Before he gave it to the people, however, what did he do first? He laid it, set it, before the Lord. He wasn't going to release something to God's people without first getting the Lord's blessing. I have struggled with this myself. I have wanted to run off and send my books to print before seeking God's approval.

The NIV changes the phrase, 'laid it up' to the word, 'deposited'. I like the word 'deposit'. This word speaks about trust. We trust our money in the bank where we deposit, right? This also tells me that we don't have to wait on the Lord to have Him deposit something into us before we write. We can write because He lives inside of us and has given us authority in this world. We can write and then deposit it before God Almighty. Some of us are still waiting for God to bring us a story or deposit something within us to write. I believe this is an either-or situation. I believe God has deposited stories within us that we don't know are already there and it takes us to start writing and search it out. He created us. He knew us before the foundations. Is it possible that the stories to be released are already in our DNA? That the stories to come out of us are our destiny?

As someone who has traveled the world speaking on writing and working with hundreds of authors, I feel that there are two routes in writing. One where we write with the authority Jesus gave us and the other to ask for stories that God wants us to write on His behalf. In both ways we are storytellers, but I do think the route of sacrificing our own stories for His stories elevates us to a Storyteller Champion. We see time and again the champions of God throughout the Bible. Look at King David and his mighty men. Look at the heroes of the faith written about in Hebrews 11. The faith chapter. They sacrificed so much.

I don't think it is something to worry about or stress about as a writer. God loves the stories I have written, and He joined me in the process of creating them and publishing them. He loves His children so much and is proud of what we do as believers here on earth. Then there are times that, if you are asking for it, then He will grant that prayer and give you a story from the vault of stories in heaven. Just write and pray. Some of the stories will be yours and then some, if you are asking for it, will be his. He will entrust a few of us to write His stories and believe me, you will know, and so will the world when they read it.

Prayer: "Lord, I bless the writers who are challenged in their heart to pull on heaven and ask to become a Storyteller Champion for you. I pray for them as they steward what you give for them to release into the world; powerful and heroic stories that will change hearts. Lord, raise up a mighty army of scribes like King David raised up his mighty men, and release them into the world. Let the stories from heaven shake the foundations of hell itself. The stories save millions of lives as their hearts turn to you. I pray that what is written by these Storyteller Champions shifts mindsets, changes cultures, and wins souls like never before. Let the darkness tremble at the sound of the keyboards tapping away. Surround these Champions with your protective angels. Bless them as they release Kingdom stories to glorify your name. Oh, I pray this prayer in Jesus' name!

Action: I wouldn't call this an action but instead a challenge. I challenge you to lay down your story when prompted by God and pray for Papa God to give you one of His stories. God works in mysterious ways, and His timing is way different than ours. You might ask and pray this, but perhaps He will wait for you to get more training, release a book or two, and then all of a sudden, He will answer that prayer. I challenge you to start praying for it now. God will set things in motion and blow your mind when the time comes to reveal it to you. Some of you are asking, "How will I know it is a story from heaven?" Oh, don't worry, you will know.

God gave me *Demons & Thieves* story ten years before my first book was ever written. I shrugged it away because I thought it was for someone else, that I wasn't qualified. After I wrote my first trilogy of epic fantasy novels and my first children's book, it happened. Interesting enough, I didn't pray ten years earlier for a story from heaven. I prayed that prayer much later and accidentally stumbled into my destiny to become a Storyteller Champion. Now, looking back, I can tell the tale. I was physically shaken by God to write the story He gave me all those years ago. I heard Him loud and clear and accepted the challenge. You see, I had to get a few books under my belt. God was training me, and I didn't even know it. He was preparing me to write the historical fiction, *Demons & Thieves*. It is only now that I can tell you not to accidentally stumble into your destiny, but instead go after it.

CHAPTER 13
KINGDOM CONFIDENCE

2 Samuel 23:20 (NLT) There was also Benaiah son of Jehoiada, a valiant warrior from Kabzeel. He did many heroic deeds, which included killing two champions of Moab. Another time, on a snowy day, he chased a lion down into a pit and killed it.

LET'S TALK ABOUT confidence for a bit.

For me, confidence didn't happen overnight. It was a lot of small victories that led me to larger victories. I needed small wins. When you look at a verse like this one, we say, "Wow, this guy is amazing. He defeated champions from other countries and even chased a lion into its home and killed it." What we don't often consider are the small victories that led to these great ones.

Benaiah didn't start off as a valiant warrior. He was a boy trying to find his way in life. He had dreams, pains, trials, tribulations, times of despair, and times of joy. Throughout his life, there were many small victories. Sometimes, just being able to wake up the next morning after losing a loved one is a victory. Don't discount what a victory looks like. All of the events in our lives shape us, hone us, develop us.

There are two types of confidence to choose from; the world's confidence or Kingdom confidence. For example, the disciples remaining in the boat is like worldly confidence. They were confident in what they knew to be true, what they experienced, etc. The disciples understood that staying in the boat was a safer option than jumping out of the boat, as there was a raging storm happening. Makes sense, right?

Then there is Kingdom confidence. Peter asks to be called out of the boat. He is called. We have big encounters with God that can (if we let them) shape us and build us up, knowing how BIG our God truly is. Prayers answered, through miracles, signs, and wonders, can truly bolster this Kingdom confidence that I speak of. It is when you step out of the equation so much so that you know you are incapable of doing whatever it is, BUT GOD can. Peter jumped out of the boat and started walking on water. That is a confidence booster.

2 Samuel 23:20 says he did "many heroic deeds," but we don't know the level of those deeds. I imagine he started out saving kittens who climbed too high up in a tree or helping an old woman walk across the street to make sure she didn't get run over by a horse or chariot. I say this in jest, but Benaiah had to start somewhere. Those small victories ultimately led him from having worldly confidence to a Kingdom confidence.

This is true with your writing. You have to start somewhere. Don't go off to a conference and expect to walk out of there knowing exactly what you need to do and write the next bestseller. Is it possible? Of course, it is, but I believe God would rather take us through the process. For one thing, it develops us as an individual. For another, He likes to walk it out with us. Remember, we co-labor with Him.

I like to say this, "Write what you know and then make up the rest." You just need to start. Write in your journal each day. Write short stories. Write poetry. Write letters to friends and family and mail them out. Write a blog. Whatever it is, just write from your heart. Whether it is seen by the public or not, it is about stepping out and obtaining those small victories.

If you pray for someone's headache and they are healed, that is an exciting victory. The next time someone comes to you with a headache, you are more confident to deal with it through prayer. Then someone comes with a migraine (which is a lot more severe than a headache). You pray, and that too is healed. Another victory! And so on and so on. Eventually, you are raising people from the dead. Now, can you start raising people from the dead, to begin with? Of course. God is the one who does it, and we step out in faith, knowing who our God is.

The same is true in our writing. We start small, and it builds. Each of my books brought me to a new level in my writing career. Not just writing, but also talking about writing, training others in writing, speaking in public, and more. Write the story given to you, steward it, and the 'more' will come until eventually you are chasing stories down into dark pits on a snowy day and killing them as a valiant warrior for the Kingdom.

My Prayer for You: "Stir up the writing warrior inside of them, Lord. Teach and equip them, Holy Spirit, to have the Kingdom confidence to go to dark places. Let them hear your voice so clearly that the sound of your voice transfers into the stories they are writing. Stir up the gift of writing inside of them. Stir up the stagnant water and turn it into living water. Let the words flow from within them. Let the words bring healing and breakthrough to those reading it. Oh, stir us up, mighty God. Let our passion for writing explode and compel us to write what you have called us to write. Call us out of the boat, Lord! Call us out! In Jesus' mighty name, amen!

Action: Write a short story about Benaiah chasing that lion down. Bring in the emotion. Let us hear what this hero was thinking, processing, remembering. Bring us into this scene as if we were there. Deep down, this will be a significant writing prompt for you as you chase down the story that calls your name. In essence, you become Benaiah and will write like a great warrior.

CHAPTER 14
TELL THE STORY

Habakkuk 2:2 (NKJV) And the Lord answered me: "Write the vision; make it plain on tablets, so he may run who reads it.

DON'T OVER COMPLICATE things. Write what you see plainly. Why? So others may not be slowed down trying to get to the core of what you mean. When they read your story, you want it to flow and keep the person running with you. If we complicate things in our storytelling, then we slow the reader down, and we may lose them.

Now, I am not saying you can't have a complicated story, especially if you are writing a mystery novel or something. I'm saying don't try to explain every single thing you are writing to the reader. Let their minds have some playtime with your words. You are the storyteller. Tell the story and let it stand on its own two feet (or three or four feet if you are writing fantasy books). Readers want to go on adventures through the storyteller's mind, or books wouldn't sell! I have seen so many writers literally stop the flow of their writing to explain to me what they meant in minute detail. And I've read books that strap me in, won't let go of me, and take me on an amazing ride.

The Holy Spirit is the best teacher. Learn from Him. He will explain truths to our hearts as we read stories, whether it be fiction or nonfiction. If God can speak through a donkey, then He sure as well can speak to us through books.

Let me ask you something, do you have to have everything in the

Bible explained to you or has the Holy Spirit shown you things on your own?

How about when you watch a "secular" movie. Doesn't God show you hidden truths within it? Or how about a "secular" book? Doesn't God reveal a comparison to His Word or remind you of something He has said to you? God is at work in <u>all</u> things! Trust Him to reveal truths that you never thought of in your writing. I absolutely love it when someone contacts me about my stories, and they proceed to tell me how a certain part affected them so much. In the back of my mind, I am blown away when I hear it because I had no intention for that to happen. I was just telling the story and letting it flow from within me.

I digress. You might be asking how the last three paragraphs have anything to do with overcomplicating things. The point I'm making is that I want you to experience freedom as a storyteller. When you are free then complications are held at bay. I want you to have laser sight vision on the tale you are weaving. When you steward the heart of a story then it flows freely from your imagination onto the paper or screen.

Let's not discount the first part of this scripture. "The Lord answered me." This means that Habakkuk prayed beforehand, and God answered his prayer. I want you to continue to lift your writing assignments up in prayer to God. Let Him bless your hands, your mind, and the story. God is faithful. He will answer your prayers, and when He does it will bring you clarity so you can write the story plain as day. You will stay on point and not be distracted.

The enemy is right there with us, however. He is trying to insert pages into the story you are telling. Over time those pages will be rejected through rewrites, beta readers, critique groups, and editing. Why? Because God will bring it to light and nothing will withstand his final edits. You will be sharpened by feedback from others like iron sharpens iron. Don't refine your work on your own. Let God co-labor with you, and He will bring in others to assist. Your job is to be praying and looking for what God is doing. Pray in the right people to read and critique your work. Pray in the wisdom to discern what is from Him and what is from the enemy.

My prayer to you: Lord, bless the storyteller reading this. I speak clarity over you in Jesus' mighty name. I speak the confidence to write the story inside of you and to stay in step with the Spirit of God. Let the words flow like a rushing river. I break off any hindrances and doubt in Jesus' name, and I thank the Lord because each word you put to paper or screen will build momentum like a wave destined to crash on a distant shore. I call the story inside of you to attention! Come out in Jesus' name. Amen!

Action: Write your prayers down in your journal, specifically targeting your writing assignment. As you read this chapter and the scripture with it, formulate your prayers and write them down. Two reasons, so you can see the prayers you wrote without having to set it to memory and then watch God answer those prayers one by one. You don't have to write only one prayer, and I suggest writing a few different ones. Be specific with God in those prayers, don't be general. Make declarations from your heart, not demanding things from God, but instead pulling on heaven. Pull-on the unseen and watch it become seen. Start visualizing your book in your hands, the thickness, the colors, the smell of the fresh ink, the book cover, your dedication, the endorsements, and so on. Declare those things! Call them out! Plunder the darkness!

SECTION THREE:
BEING A STORYTELLER CHAMPION

Unleashing the Storyteller Within You

CAN WE CREATE stories that will have generations talking about them long after we are gone?

Are we dreaming about that kind of impact?

Is that at the forefront of our minds as we release our books?

When I first started dreaming of becoming a famous author, it wasn't dreaming about future generations coming after me to read my work. It wasn't anything further than me making a lot of money and entertaining those in front of me. I had no idea or concept of generational momentum. It wasn't even a thought. It was all about me and what I get *now*. It took many years walking with God to unravel my mindset, and even still, He continues to show me deeper truths.

When I speak at conferences or workshops, I am always challenging the audience to think of these things. To think higher than themselves. To think of the kids coming after them. To not limit our thinking to the here and now but instead the future beyond ourselves.

Did you know that there are stories in heaven waiting to be released? I didn't either. That is until I started asking God what stories He wanted to tell. Once you start asking Him (instead of telling Him the stories you are going to write), then it's a whole new ballgame.

We are a story-driven world. We are a story-driven people. We are constantly looking for the next story. Everything we do has a story tied to it, and as we go about our day, new narratives are developing. We usually tell those stories around the water cooler at work or at the dinner table with friends and family.

When someone asks, "How are you doing?" it is an invitation to tell a tale, and the person asking is open and waiting. Sometimes our stories aren't that good. But then there are the times we release a whopper of a tale that is retold not just by you but by others. The same is true for our writings. Quite often there are a lot of books released that are, to be honest, not that good. Then there are the bestsellers that lock themselves in a special spot created by our hearts to hold on to for the rest of our lives.

Let's go after the bestsellers.

Let's represent the King and His Kingdom well.

Let's not let the lure of the bestseller be a distraction.

The joy of the Lord is our strength, and whether we write something that isn't good in the eyes of this world or we write a bestseller, we do it all for the glory of God. He is all that matters, not the recognition of man.

God considers our work for Him the best! Write with a smile on your face knowing how God sees you.

CHAPTER 15
#1 BESTSELLER

2 Timothy 3:16-17 (TPT) Every Scripture has been written by the Holy Spirit, the breath of God. It will empower you by its instruction and correction, giving you the strength to take the right direction and lead you deeper into the path of godliness. Then you will be God's servant, fully mature and perfectly prepared to fulfill any assignment God gives you.

GOD's WORD HAS been the #1 bestseller of all time every year to this very day.

The Bible is fascinating. Just look and ponder the contents. There are 66 books in the Bible comprised of 39 books from the Old Testament and 27 books in the New Testament.

The Full Bible has been translated to over 500 languages and the New Testament--over 2,800! That is incredible! How many of us would even dream of having our work translated into another language outside of what we wrote?

Let me break down the Bible for you a little more:

It took 1,500 years to write it.

There were 40 contributing writers.

These writers spanned over 40 generations.

These writers, over the course of their lives, held 20 different occupations.

It was written in 10 countries.

Those countries were spread across 6k miles.

And there is only 1 author. GOD!

Those few details alone are incredible. We complain when our work takes over a year to complete, and that is just one writer on just one project. Now consider the forty different writers. I could give forty people a subject to write about today (even the same story with characters and everything else). And I can tell you, *every single one* of those forty people would bring back a completely different sounding piece than the rest. Nothing would sound the same. Nothing would read the same. And yet when we read the Bible, from Genesis to Revelation, we hear the *same* voice. We hear the author. That is powerful.

There is more.

There are 2,930 different characters mentioned in 1,551 geographical scenes of action. That is *a lot* of character development. The Bible contains every conceivable subject in every literary form (poetry, prose, romance, mystery, biography, science, history, etc.). The Bible is 75% story, 15% poetry, and 10% instruction.

I like to look at it this way: 75% story, 15% poetry, and 100% instruction. There is instruction in the stories and poetry, right?

The Bible was the first book to ever be printed in the year 1454 and has sold over 6 billion copies. God's word has been the #1 bestseller of all time every year to this very day. It sells 50 copies per minute. That's right, a minute. Sixty seconds pass, and fifty copies have been sold.

Let's look at music. In the world today, over 1 million songs are released each year. I don't think I need to tell you, these are not all good songs. The majority of them are bringing hate and division. Don't get me wrong, the songs have a happy, upbeat, very catchy tune. BUT if you stop for a moment and review the lyrics, you will see that everyone who repeats them, including our children, are singing hate and division all over themselves.

The power of storytelling will influence people, culture, societies, nations, the world.

Let's look at one of the most impactful industries out there. Movies. There has been a 30% increase in movie theaters being built around the world with ten a day in China alone. TEN a day! Wow! Why? Movies shift things. Again, we are story-driven people. We can't get enough, and movies is a quick and easy way to get us there. The average person spends 4 to 5 hours a day watching television. It is literally a drug, and we are hooked on the drug called 'story'.

Every year twenty-thousand movies are released worldwide.

3,500 of those are released in America.

Of those 3,500, only 700 make it to theaters.

150 of those 700 make more than 5 million dollars.

31 of those 150 make more than 100 million dollars. We call these blockbusters.

The highest-grossing movie of all time, once you calculate inflation, is *Gone With The Wind*. It has grossed $3,440,000,000 so far, and it came out January 17th, 1940. *Avatar*, *Star Wars*, and *Titanic* follow close behind.

We quote movies almost daily. Movie quotes have become part of our vocabulary, and there is meaning behind the quotes we say. I remember a book signing at the San Diego Festival of Books. There were over ten-thousand attendees and vendors, and the place was so packed it was hard to get by people. One lady was trying to get through the crowd, and she looked over at me and said, "We are going to need a bigger boat."

That one line conveyed everything she felt to me, and it is a movie quote from *Jaws*. This is just one example. Take a moment to briefly inventory all of your movie one-liners. Take a moment to see everyone around you say their own movie one-liners. These are all from stories that have "influenced" us.

Now, let's take a look at books. Anywhere from 600 thousand to 1 million books are released each year. That is a lot of books. That is a lot of stories! But once again, not a lot of those stories are good.

While researching, I discovered something very fascinating. A location. It amazed me so much that I needed to go to that place, and bring a team of other writers with me. It is what is known as a Writer's Retreat. But we call it a Writer's Advance because we don't retreat from anything. We advance! We took a team to the United Kingdom, more specifically, Oxford. This place is magical. A thin veil to heaven for creativity.

Why?

Authors have left their imprint on the place. Scribes have touched heaven and released their books in this place. Nine books have sold over 100M copies, and several of these giants originated from Oxford. Here are a few based upon information on Wikipedia.

- Charles Dickens book, *Tale of Two Cities*, has over 200 million copies sold. Written in London, England in 1859. London is a little over 50 miles away from Oxford.

- JRR Tolkien's book *Lord Of The Rings,* sold over 150 million copies. Written in Oxford, UK.

- JK Rowling's book *Harry Potter and the Philosophers Stone* sold over 120 million and her entire series sold over 510 million. Written in England and Scotland.

- JRR Tolkien's book *The Hobbit* sold 100 million. Written in Oxford, UK.

- Lewis Carroll's book *Alice and Wonderland* sold 100 million. Written in Oxford, UK.

- CS Lewis' *Chronicles of Narnia* series sold over 120 million. Written in Oxford, UK.

- Agatha Christie's book *And Then There Were None* sold over 100 million. Written in Oxfordshire, UK, which is only six minutes from Oxford.

Are you getting it? Do you see the pattern?

We took a team to Oxford in 2017 and had a life-changing experience walking the streets of these literary greats. Also, did you notice that there are no authors from the USA? Now, we have many literary giants from the states, but no one selling a single book to the degree we see here above.

San Diego has a rich background of authors and books, and I strongly feel that San Diego will be the Hollywood for Writers.

Theodor Seuss Geisel, known by everyone as Dr. Seuss, wrote 42 books that sold over 600 million copies. He is considered the 9th best selling fiction author of all time. He lived in San Diego.

Tim Lahaye, author of the *Left Behind* series, sold over 80 million copies worldwide. It consisted of sixteen books. He lived in San Diego.

Frank L. Baum wrote most of his *Oz* series while in San Diego at the Coronado Hotel.

Raymond E. Feist is a graduate of UCSD and has sold over 15 million copies of his fantasy Riftwar War Cycle series. He lives in San Diego.

There are many other notable figures writing great works in San Diego. Several have gone to be made into feature films, such as *Heaven Is For Real* and *Same Kind of Different As Me*, both written by Lynn Vincent. Her books have also sold millions of copies.

Not only does San Diego have a rich depth of authors but also playwrights. Did you know that San Diego is a city that has sent more plays to Broadway than any other city? That's right. Over 50 plays have gone to Broadway in the last 30 years. Major successes such as *Into the Woods*, *Jersey Boys*, and *The Full Monty*, to name a few.

Let me get back to Oxford. Kingdom Writers Association plans on continuing to take teams to Oxford. There is something strong about going to places where great breakthrough has occurred. And in the storytelling world, Oxford is one of those places. It appears that San Diego is another.

I think the coming and going between the two will create an amazing synergy of pulling on Heaven and releasing those stories here on Earth.

To recap, we live in a story-driven world. Period.

Why did I give you all of this amazing information? Well, I wanted to end on this one piece of scripture. It is found in the book of Ephesians and the scripture used is also a dedicated chapter in this devotional worth repeating again here.

Ephesians 5:1 *"**Imitate God**, therefore, **in everything you do**, because you are his dear children."*

Wait. What? Did God just challenge us as writers? Did he just say copy Him? Yes, He did.

What does that mean for you and me?

As writers, God is telling us to imitate Him in everything we do. God is the best selling author of all time. He is calling to us to also become the bestselling author of all time. Whatever God does, we can also do. Don't limit things to only healing the sick or raising the dead or casting out demons, but realize God is also an author, the best author, even an author of faith, our faith.

Don't over-analyze this. Don't carry the weight of this word. Let peace reign inside of you. Understand that you are called as a scribe for the Kingdom. Pursue excellence, don't pursue perfection. Let the Holy Spirit be your guide and write with God. A word like this can paralyze people as the enemy whispers into your ear, "You don't have what it takes."

God has what it takes, and He resides inside of you. Just be you, but be you fully alive in Jesus. Do that, and see where it takes you.

Bilbo Baggins said it best, "I'm going on an adventure!"

It is time for us as writers to be the explorers of the unknown and go on crazy adventures with God. Are you ready? Are you yelling inside yourself, "Here I am. Send me!" I say yes and amen, too!

Now, it is time to unleash the Storyteller Champion inside of you. God is the ultimate storyteller, and He is inside of you as a believer. So when I say, unleash the storyteller within you, our instant go-to is ourselves, but in reality, we are giving God permission to bust out and co-labor with us to pour out the stories from heaven that have never been heard before.

Ask, and you shall receive.

Prayer: "Lord, I ask in your name, for the mighty stories within heaven to be revealed to us. Send us the triumph over tragedy, the love that conquers hate, the impossible to be possible. We want to partner with you to change lives, to point the readers back to you supernaturally, and for you to capture their heart from the darkness of this world. Let us be your voice in this time, in this place, in this hour. Let us be your storyteller champions in Jesus' name!"

Action: Brainstorm with God. Pray the above prayer, repeat it if necessary, and start writing down everything you hear, see, touch, or taste in your mind's eye. It might be a question you have. Questions turn into stories as you go after the answer. It might be visuals that you can't explain like the creatures Ezekiel witnessed or what the Apostle John saw in Revelation. Whatever it is, write it down. Keep pressing in for the stories in the vault of heaven. If you don't get a story now, you might get it ten years later. Your prayer that you prayed now might be answered later.

CHAPTER 16
WHY TELL STORIES?

Matthew 13:10-15 (MSG) The disciples came up and asked, "Why do you tell stories?"
He replied, "You've been given insight into God's kingdom. You know how it works. Not everybody has this gift, this insight; it hasn't been given to them. Whenever someone has a ready heart for this, the insights and understandings flow freely. But if there is no readiness, any trace of receptivity soon disappears. That's why I tell stories: to create readiness, to nudge the people toward receptive insight.

A STORY TILLS THE ground of someone's heart to prepare it for a seed of truth to be planted.

Why Tell Stories?

The why's of storytelling:

1. To bring truth (it's a carrier of hope—a messenger)

2. To open hearts to truth (prepares a heart to receive truth)

3. To set captive hearts free (break the chains of those in prison)

4. To heal hearts (heal the sick)

Sounds like the gospel message to me, doesn't it? We bring good news, and through that good news, hearts receive the love of Jesus, captives are set free, people are healed. And we *should* be. We should be following the Master Storyteller, Jesus, who spoke in riddles to those that gathered. He prayed that they would have ears to hear and eyes to see what he was imparting, but he never gave the masses explanations of his parables. Why? Because he was "creating readiness" within their hearts to receive the truth. Without truth seeping into our heart it will be like seed thrown onto hard ground where the birds will quickly snatch it away. We need to simply tell our story without explaining everything to our readers. I think as Christians we have been programmed to teach and explain every sermon we have heard. This bleeds over into our storytelling. Take the story you have been given and tell it. Take the reader on an amazing journey that creates a readiness within them toward receptive insight.

Here is a bit of science behind storytelling. Stories activate our entire brain while information only activates a part of the brain. If I give you only the bullet-point information, then it only hits your language processing part of the brain where we decode words into meaning (nothing else).

But if I share a story with that same bullet-point information, your brain sets ablaze with light. A story not only ignites the language processing section but also any other part of the brain where the story experience reaches. For example, think about someone telling you about food or riding a roller coaster in a story format. Your brain is firing on many cylinders throughout the story as it relates to your own personal experience. If I gave you just information about food or a roller coaster and how it works, then just your language processor is on.

Why tell stories? We get more with stories. We can plant ideas, thoughts, and emotions into other's brains. There is an impartation we release to someone experiencing the story we give them.

Whenever we hear a story, we instantly want to relate it to one of our existing experiences. Jesus knew what He was doing when He went around telling stories instead of telling bullet-point information about the Kingdom. As storytellers ourselves, let's tap into that. Can you give your revelatory information through a story? Yes, you can!

Prayer: "Lord, Jesus, I bless everyone reading this book and being inspired in their calling as your Kingdom Scribe. I pray right now that they can formulate their real-life experiences into amazing stories. Help them take the dark spots in their life and fold it into a fictionalized story. Help them bring the truth of the event into a character and fantasy adventure. Let their stories ignite and open hearts to the truth of who you are. Amen."

Action: Read Matthew 13: 10-15 through several versions. Pray afterward to receive revelation from the Holy Spirit about storytelling. Write what you hear into your journal.

CHAPTER 17
THE PEN OF A SKILLFUL WRITER

Psalm 45:1 (NIV) "My heart is stirred by a noble theme as I recite my verses for the king; my tongue is the pen of a skillful writer."

HAVE YOU EVER been sleeping to only be awakened suddenly with a story in your mind? Have you been driving along and then a flash of a scene enters your thoughts?

These are stirrings from God. It is our job as scribes to search out and steward them. Our hearts are stirred by the Most High, and when we write, we write with His truth at the core, whether fiction or nonfiction.

Look at the second part of this verse. "I recite my verses for the king." If we can't read our story aloud to the King, then we should take another look at our writing. What an honor to read our work before the Lord. Do you not want to be prepared to do such a thing? Would someone not practice before seeing the King?

The last part of this speaks volumes. "My tongue is the pen of a skillful writer." We need to be constantly training and equipping ourselves to become that skillful writer. Early on, I thought I was the best writer out there, even before I published my first book. I know, I'm probably the only one, right? Some say that it is built-in confidence, but others would say it is arrogance. I agree with both.

There is a maturity to our walk with the Lord. With each step we take, we learn and grow, constantly maturing. Psalms 45:1 uses a keyword: IS! My tongue *is.* That is a powerful statement. Some might say that is confidence or arrogance. We need to work to become skillful writers. But, at the same time, we must "declare" in our hearts that we *are* skillful writers. God does something supernatural within us when we declare things. Remember, we are not of this world, so break off the thought of arrogance and step into your calling as a son/daughter of God and confidently pull on your inheritance. We didn't earn this inheritance. It was given to us. It is time for us to show up. Our confidence comes from the Lord because of what He has done, not what we have done.

Now, how do we discern confidence and arrogance? Arrogance is when you are telling everyone you meet what a great writer you are or that you are a skillful writer. Confidence is when, in private, you are declaring to your flesh and spirit that YOU ARE a skillful and talented writer. One provokes arrogance, and the other strengthens you as a person to step into your calling as a Kingdom Scribe. Do you see the difference? If not then try it out and see how you feel from each experience. When you are out with your friends. Talk about how good you are as a writer. See how you feel after that. Then try the other in private.

I say this in jest. You probably don't have to try it out, and I suggest not to, but I wanted to get the point across.

When you declare a thing, it matters. You will become a better writer in conjunction with declarations along with honing your skills with practical training.

Prayer: "Papa God, it is time for your scribal army to be awakened. It is time for them to take their place. Help them understand who they are. Strengthen their mind and heart and let their faith be bolstered like never before. Protect them from the whispers of darkness that say they are not good enough. You say they are good enough and that is all that matters. Lord, bless your scribes and let us rise up and release our writings into the world to change hearts and glorify your name."

Action: Stand in front of the mirror and declare three times, increasing in volume, the following out loud, "I am a skillful writer!"

CHAPTER 18
WRITE WITH CERTAINTY

Romans 5:1-5 (TPT) Our faith in Jesus transfers God's righteousness to us and he now declares us flawless in his eyes. This means we can now enjoy true and lasting peace with God, all because of what our Lord Jesus, the Anointed One, has done for us. Our faith guarantees us permanent access into this marvelous kindness that has given us a perfect relationship with God. What incredible joy bursts forth within us as we keep on celebrating our hope of experiencing God's glory!
But that's not all! Even in times of trouble we have a joyful confidence, knowing that our pressures will develop in us patient endurance. And patient endurance will refine our character, and proven character leads us back to hope. And this hope is not a disappointing fantasy, because we can now experience the endless love of God cascading into our hearts through the Holy Spirit who lives in us!

WRITE WITH CERTAINTY.
Our life should be anchored in our certainty because we follow a God of certainty.

The Lord brought me to read these verses for a few weeks. Each time I marveled at what the Word was telling me, what it was reminding me, what I needed to hear. This scripture shares so much. Look at the keywords such as "declares us flawless in his eyes," and "our faith guarantees us permanent access into his marvelous kindness." Come on! This is incredible! Then look at verse 3, "But that's not all!"

What I want to tell you is write with certainty, write like the disciples penned the Bible. Let the Holy Spirit flow through you onto paper.

I never imagined myself being a ghostwriter until *Demons & Thieves* was produced. God literally instructed me the entire way through it, telling me what to write. Like the disciples were instructed on what to write for the Bible, I was instructed to write a work of historical fiction. In the editing process, we discovered the sections where I tried to bring in my influence, and they were eliminated.

It is an honor to write for the Lord.

You are a scribal Ambassador to the Kingdom of Heaven. You bring glorious news to a darkened world. You bring a battering ram of joy to those with hardened faces of sadness. You drop love grenades through the written word. And every person who buys your book or reads your words experience the explosion upon their soul.

Just writing this got me all fired up!

If God has called you to write, then write. Nothing should separate you from that calling. And when you are called by God, then we should lean into Him and not withhold anything back. Much like the chapter where I spoke about Jesus saying, "Let's go to the other side," we can bank on it that God is going to come through for us as writers with the assignment He has given us. Once we get a hold of this truth then we can write with certainty.

Let's stop fighting the internal battles of how we are not worthy, we are incapable, we don't have time, I have to work, I have a family, I am sick, I am tired, and all the other excuses we come up with. The "I can't" statement must end for us to move forward.

Let's write with confidence and joy. We have nothing to lose and everything to gain. You must steel yourself to the point that no matter if anyone ever reads your work, it doesn't matter because you wrote it for the Lord and you followed through on your assignment. Yes, we want readers, but get yourself so aligned with God's calling that all that counts is His approval, not man's.

If He is for you, then who can be against you? If He has called you to write something, then let nothing stand in your way of completing that assignment. Still the storms, cast aside the demons who step in your way, strengthen your mind, and GO FOR IT!

My prayer to writers reading this: Lord, ignite the destined writer inside. Stir their heart awake. Flood their minds with your thoughts and ideas. Let the ink flow out onto paper like the Holy Spirit flows out of man. Release Kingdom revelation to them in their dreams, as they drive, while they shower. Equip them to go higher with you and be able to take on more and more as you develop them. Come, Holy Spirit, and invade broken mindsets and broken ideas that don't align with your truths. Set their feet back on the path you have blazed for them. Let the words pour out, let the stories come down from heaven, delivered on wings of angels.

I declare peace over you now in Jesus name. I declare laser-sharp focus to come upon you and the wisdom to use that focus as the Lord directs you. I pray all of this in Jesus' mighty name. Amen!

Action: I want you to pray and ask Papa God what part of your writing you want to share. Take just a piece of your writing. It could be a few sentences or a paragraph and post it onto one or several of your social media platforms. Facebook is usually a good place. Put it out there. See the feedback you get from it. Only do as God directs you. You might feel nothing at first. Pray and then read through some of your work. God will nudge you, and in the back of your mind you will hear, "That's it. Post that part." You will even think it was your own voice. Just go with it.

In this action, you are listening to God first. Don't post anything without His direction. Then sit back, don't hover over your posting, check on it periodically, and watch what God does with it. You followed His direction. That is all that matters. This action is training you towards His affections.

What happens if no one responds? What happens if someone says something negative? It doesn't matter. Remember, you follow His voice, and you already have His approval. This is training you in a small way as you go further and deeper into your calling as a writer to get His approval before anything. And once you have His approval, nothing else matters.

CHAPTER 19
PROPHETIC WRITING

Revelation 1:19 (ESV) Write therefore the things that you have seen, those that are and those that are to take place after this.

I CALL THIS PROPHETIC writing.
I love being led to scriptures like this one. Take a look at this with me. Let's explore it together. It starts off "write therefore." It's a command. Write what you have seen, what you have experienced, what you have lived.

This verse starts off with a command, "Write." And here's how the dots connect (therefore). Write the things you have seen. Write what has happened, what is happening, and here is the kicker, what WILL happen.

You will find yourself writing about things that have not happened yet (and this applies to fiction writers just as much). How many sci-fi books have been thought to be impossible ideas or concepts to only have them happened in our lifetime?

God will show us things to write about. He will recall memories that were once dormant and long-forgotten inside of us. Take note of those moments. God will also show us things that are to take place. A future event. Take note of these and pray into it. A wise man seeks counsel so go to your prayer warriors, your pastor, your trusted friend and share your thoughts. Get confirmation as you write prophetic statements.

If you are a fiction writer, pray into how God wants you to release your word, and then let the story attach itself to your heart as you pour it out onto paper or screen.

Have fun exploring with God. Have amazing encounters with Him that made you and formed you and destined you to be here in this time and in this place reading this book.

Prophetic writing doesn't have to be intense or stressful. Let me give you an example. You might have a main character in your story that really depicts you. You are writing this character as if you were that character. During your writing, you show us that this character is a famous author who has just surpassed the sales of JK Rowling (*Harry Potter*) and is dealing with the emotions of just months ago living in their car on the streets and now looking out from a penthouse suite to the city lights glowing below.

Let this scene be prophetic writing for yourself and your future. Don't just write a cool story but impart things to you and to those reading it. Call things out prophetically.

The definition of "prophetic" - accurately describing or predicting what will happen in the future. God has given us this gift, and He wants us to eagerly desire these gifts. But remember, this gift is to edify and encourage the Body of Christ.

1 Corinthians 14:1 "Follow the way of love and eagerly desire gifts of the Spirit, especially prophecy."

Pray this prayer: "Lord, show me things. Reveal to me things that have not been seen or heard."

Action: Pray this prayer, and then sit quietly, listening for ten minutes. Afterward, write down what He showed you in your journal. Even if you didn't see or hear anything just start writing anyways. I find that God will show me things as I write. Start by writing your feelings or any thought that comes to mind and let it flow without editing. Do this until you feel inside of you it is time to stop writing. Then read through what you wrote. God will highlight something to you. It could be an idea for your next book. You never know.

CHAPTER 20
SALES VS. SOULS

Colossians 3:23 (ESV) Whatever you do, work heartily, as for the Lord and not for men...

I T'S UNFORTUNATE THAT many Kingdom writers follow what man is looking for instead of what God is.

I've seen it time and time again. I'm at a Christian author gathering, and many writers are talking about the latest buzz and what they should write about to garner more sales. They even try to bring you into their conversation by asking you what you do about getting sales. The question isn't bad, but it is the motive that you feel behind it. It's kind of like a Pastor of a church being asked by everyone how many people attend their church. We live in comparison to numbers. If I tell you my book has only sold 10 copies so far then you might turn to someone else who has sold 1,000 copies and give them more interest. Why? Because in our flesh we want to be successful and in our flesh we see 10 sold books as a failure and 1,000 books sold as a success. We fully discount the story behind the sales.

Let's go a little deeper with this 10 to 1,000 comparison. We don't know what God is doing. With the person rejected by so many because of his dismal sales, we didn't realize that a young boy was one of the 10 people who read it and he ends up becoming the next Billy Graham or CS Lewis, contributing his success to this book. And because of this boy's success and now talking about this book that only sold 10 copies, it now is selling millions of copies. We then compare the other book that sold 1,000 copies, and it hadn't sold anything else but a few hundred more.

I say this because I have been there and done that in regards to comparison. I have even been one to tote my own sales to try and be someone in other's eyes. God has been speaking to me more and more that it doesn't matter about the sales. The only thing that matters is God. What does He say? What does He desire? What does He want to do with this writing assignment He has placed upon you?

As a believer, we need to shift our mindset to that of asking God what He wants us to write about and not what the world wants. I think God knows what He is doing. Don't you?

The more we align ourselves with Him, the better off we will be.

Our motive shouldn't be about the sales, but instead about the *souls*. Our attitude as Christians needs to change, for we are not of this world. We write from a perspective that is not really our own. We write to affect the generations coming behind us. We write to bring about change in our world. We write to stir the hearts of men. We write to bring God glory, not ourselves.

Prayer: Lord, let us have peace about the calling you have placed on our lives. Let us stay focused on you and not the water we walk upon nor the storms that surround us. Let us stay in step with you, Holy Spirit. Guide us, teach us, show us the way that you want us to go. Lead us not into temptation, but deliver us from evil. Deliver us from our flesh that wants to thrive in greed and lust as authors. Remind us that fame is not bad, but it must come from you as part of our assignment. Let us steward fame as Kingdom Writers to glorify you and not ourselves. Bring us favor and influence that we can use to make you famous. We love you, God. We love everything about you. We do what we are called to do out of love. And we thank you for first loving us. Bless our writing. Bless our assignment and may our writings reach the people you have destined us to reach in the wonderful and powerful name of Jesus we pray, amen!

Action: Get a ziplock bag big enough to hold your manuscript or book or whatever it is your writing. You could even print out the title and what it is about if you haven't started anything yet. Just have something that symbolizes your project in the bag.

Now, go and fill your sink with water. Doesn't matter if it is warm or cold water. You don't have to fill it all the way but at least halfway. Make sure the bag is fully sealed. Anoint your bag with oil (if you have it). Olive oil will work just fine. Pray over your assignment. Take a moment to be heartfelt about the calling as a Kingdom Writer that God has placed upon you.

Take your bag and baptize it in the name of the Father, the Son, and the Holy Spirit. Dedicate your assignment to God and thank Him for what He is breathing in and through you.

Lastly, take a picture of you holding your bag up dripping with water. Let it be a reminder to you. Print it out and keep it posted at your workstation or somewhere that you can see it often. Capture the moment. Let it be a stone of remembrance.

CHAPTER 21
EMBRACE HIS STORY

Luke 9:23 (TPT) Jesus said to all of his followers, "If you truly desire to be my disciple, you must disown your life completely, embrace my 'cross' as your own, and surrender to my ways.

THERE IS NO bottom to the depth of this statement, but I want to give you a new perspective on this. Remember, I'm looking at this with a writer's lens. If we really want to learn from Jesus, then we MUST disengage from our own stories COMPLETELY and embrace HIS stories as our own.

What?

In the beginning, we have our stories to tell. Of justice, of willpower, of experience--and they are all great stories. But, let's be honest and look deep within ourselves. The current tale you are weaving comes, in part, from God. There is also a lot of you, as there should be. God loves you and wants to join you in your storytelling, so there is nothing wrong with that. Go for it.

BUT, what this verse says to me is that there is another way of imparting stories into this world. That is His way—completely surrendering ourselves to His process.

I wrote three epic fantasy novels and a children's book before realizing this truth. I started asking this question in my prayer time, "God, what story do you want me to tell? Is there something that you want to release through me?" The answer was always yes, but He was waiting for me to ask it.

God gave me one of His stories years before I ever published my first book. At the time, I thought it was a story for someone else to tell because it was out of my comfort zone. It was outside my genre. It wasn't the story I wanted to tell. *Demons & Thieves* is all His. Yes, I co-labored to write it, but the story was all His. And what an AMAZING story it is. It is hard to believe I penned it. It is hard to believe He entrusted it to me.

I encourage you to get your story out. Just write! And when you are ready (and I mean really ready), then you can pray the prayer below. Embracing His cross (His story) is an incredible privilege, so prepare your heart, mind, soul, strength to surrender your ways and be fully committed to Him.

Prayer: "Lord, what story would you like me to tell on your behalf? Let me be your Storyteller Champion and write the story you want to tell. Commission me, Lord. Here I am, send it to me."

Action: Write in your journal what you hear from God after praying. Spend quite a bit of quiet time listening. You might have to be the persistent widow and continue to ask for the story. Keep writing what you hear. You will know when He gives you the story because it will be beyond anything you could have imagined on your own.

SECTION FOUR
IMPARTATIONS

CHAPTER 22
ADDISON'S WALK- OXFORD, UK SEPTEMBER 2017

As writers, we are pioneers in all respects.

Why?

Because we are going into places we have never been before and sharing what we experienced while there. We go to foreign worlds, visit new creations, new people, and even discover new things about ourselves.

One of my dreams was to go to Oxford, United Kingdom. I wanted to walk the streets of the legendary pioneers JRR Tolkien and CS Lewis. We launched Kingdom Writers Association in 2016, and by the end of that year, I was working on how to get to Oxford. In my mind and heart, I was set to go, not knowing any of the logistics of what it would take.

But God!

The Holy Spirit started lining everything up. As I moved forward, my focus shifted from just me and my wife going, to wondering who else would want to go with me on this crazy adventure. That is when the Writer's Retreat came to the forefront. It quickly changed to Writers Advance as I strongly felt (and still feel) that our words matter and the word 'retreat' just didn't sound right.

We don't retreat, we advance!

We teamed up with another writing group led by Dr. Mark Stibbe, who runs Kingdom Writing Solutions in the UK. Together, we formed an 'Advance' that I feel will be difficult to duplicate. It truly set the bar really high, namely because it was the first time any of us had done such a thing. A lot of work went into the coordination from all sides. Without Mark and his amazing wife Cherith, it would have been difficult to pull off on my own.

One of the things at the top of our list was walking "Addison's Walk" located on the campus of Magdalen College. It is a picturesque footpath around a small island along the River Cherwell. This is a special place as it is expressed that CS Lewis, JRR Tolkien, and Hugo Dyson were walking the path together talking about God, metaphors, and myth, and they had a wonderful experience. Here are the words from CS Lewis to a friend just two days after the occurrence.

"We began (in Addison's walk just after dinner) on metaphor and myth—interrupted by a rush of wind which came so suddenly on the still, warm evening and sent so many leaves pattering down that we thought it was raining. We all held our breath, the other two appreciating the ecstasy of such a thing almost as you would. We continued (in my room) on Christianity: a good long satisfying talk in which I learned a lot: then discussed the difference between love and friendship — then finally drifted back to poetry and books." – *Letter to Arthur Greeves Sept 22nd, 1931*

Interesting that it was September 2017--around the same season as when Lewis went to Addison's Walk in his group in 1931, 86 years prior. We had already spent days in Oxford with a special day of touring planned. That day, our group coordinated to see several key locations. This was our final stop for the day, and we truly saved the best for last. I remember seeing everything leading up to this point in my mind. The famous Blackwell bookshop, Pembroke College where JRR Tolkien taught for twenty years, Bodleian Library, the home of CS Lewis, the grave of both men. But at the top of my mind and heart was getting to this significant place with our group. I can't tell you why, but there was a strong pulling to be there. I *needed* to be there. One of the things I told the KWA members before we left the USA was that I was going to Oxford, and I wouldn't return without a limp. I was going to get something from God out there, and I would wrestle Him for it, much as Jacob did.

Dr. Mark Stibbe and I found a good spot on the path. There were landscaping dreamscapes with trees, the river, and beauty all around us. Mark said to me, "Brae, why don't you say a few words and pray."

I hadn't much thought of saying anything other than this is a very special place, and I couldn't truly wrap my mind around the fact that I was actually there. I said a few words explaining the significance of that place, and then I read the part of CS Lewis' letter where he described the rush of wind that came suddenly. I started to pray and became overwhelmed with the Holy Spirit. I felt strongly it was time to listen, so I instructed everyone to just focus on God and listen to what He had to say to each of us individually.

We were in a Holy silence, and then the wind rushed in suddenly, blowing through the trees. It sounded like rushing water. And then we heard large drops as if someone threw stones into the river behind us. It subsided after a minute, and we all looked up at one another in awe. Each of us started sharing what we heard and saw with Papa God during that time.

"What was the sound we heard?" I asked. John Spencer from the UK team said, "It was seeds falling from the trees into the river." He went on to tell us the significance of those seeds as they fell. They drop into the water and are carried downstream where they will be planted further away, and a new tree will be birthed. It was an example of what and who we are as writers. God's message to us was clear. We are His scribes, and our writing becomes the seeds that are taken around the world and cause new life to be birthed.

Each of us found a seed and took it home as a reminder of what happened that day. My seed is in my office inside a special display case that harbors items I've collected from several locations in Oxford from this amazing life-changing trip. It is my reminder of the message God imparted to us on Addison's Walk.

Your writing is a tree. That tree is creating and releasing seeds that are falling and traveling to new places, being planted to create more trees. It is a beautiful picture. Grab hold of it.

Prayer: I pray a special travel blessing on those reading this prayer. Lord, bless them by opening up doors for them to travel around the world to places like Oxford or to Israel. I pray this favor and blessing in Jesus' mighty name. Amen!

Action: As a Kingdom Scribe, I highly encourage you to take a pilgrimage to Oxford. It is a thin place for writers. I plan on taking teams periodically out there so you can contact me if you want to see if it lines up with your schedule. Contact me for our next departure date.

www.KingdomWritersAssociation.com

CHAPTER 23
IMPARTATIONS AND MANTLES

Romans 1:11 (NIV) I long to see you so that I may impart to you some spiritual gift to make you strong—

IMMEDIATELY AFTER OUR first trip to Oxford in 2017, my wife and I embarked on a personal vacation and adventure to Scotland. Our last day in Scotland, we entered the city of Edinburgh with a focused destination. We wanted to visit the same restaurant that JK Rowling wrote most of *Harry Potter: The Philosopher's Stone.* The Elephant House is widely known now due to her incredible success with the book series.

We entered the establishment, and my wife asked if we could be seated where she sat. Now, I thought that was probably not going to happen, but the waiter smiled and said, "Follow me." He brought us to the exact table, confirmed by us from interviews she had that we had watched. Out the window, it overlooked the castle. We ate breakfast, we prayed, and we wrote in our journals. Below is what I wrote in my journal, word for word without editing.

May what we received by being there be passed along and multiplied through each of you reading this. I pray the storyteller inside of you is unleashed in Jesus' name.

9/21/17 The Elephant House in Edinburgh, Scotland

I sit in the spot of one who wrote the series that changed the world. I am eating breakfast while an ancient castle sits outside my window idly by, waiting for us to enter its gates. I am watching my bride soak in the atmosphere of this now notable figure; now penning her own prose. Can one truly grasp the thought and mind of an individual by visiting the very locations they resided? Only God grants the desires of those searching for Him. Through this adventure, we travel with the Traveler of travelers, and it is by His stripes that our stories flow. What stories will be birthed from our meager visit in this foreign land under the umbrella of a not so foreign artwork of book writing? I can't wait to find out.

9/21/17 The Elephant House in Edinburgh, Scotland

Stories flow, stories flow

Let the light of the letters glow

Your spirit resides deep inside

To the recesses of my very mind

Bring out the stories of old

The stories of gold

Where impurities bow

And the truth revealed does not cow

Stories flow, stories flow

Let the light of the letters glow

Prayer: "Lord Jesus, I pray an impartation of storytelling upon those reading this prayer. Let their stories shine brighter than before. Let their tales of intrigue bring the reader deeper and closer to you. Ignite a fire inside of the storyteller that never diminishes, that never goes out, that never waivers. I impart a supernatural blessing to you right now in Jesus name. Let all that I flow in as a writer fill you right now in Jesus name. Holy Spirit, invade every aspect of their writing. Seep into the cracks of their imagination in Jesus name."

Action: Take some time to research your city and find out who has been a successful writer. Find out the history of your city in regards to writing. Stir up ancient wells that nobody knows about or talks about. There are things left behind in the spirit realm for us as believers to discover. Pray with Papa God and have Him lead you in your adventure of discovery. Pray and ask for impartations left behind.

CHAPTER 24
SUPERNATURAL WRITINGS

Acts 19:11-12 (NIV) God did extraordinary miracles through Paul, so that even handkerchiefs and aprons that had touched him were taken to the sick, and their illnesses were cured and the evil spirits left them.

W E WILL NEVER fully know the depth of our book's influence. We will never see all of where or how our books got to certain places and opened the eyes of the reader in that place and time.

You might be thinking this is an odd verse for a writer's devotional but I assure you that it isn't. We see in this scripture that there is a supernatural transfer or impartation that happens with believers to others who come in contact with that particular item.

These kinds of happenings are found throughout the Bible. And it is no different with our writing. Are we not healed and set free by the words we read in the Bible?

Why?

The Bible you are reading now was printed on a press somewhere in the world, packaged, stored, shipped, just like billions of others. So why is your Bible any more special than the others? It's not on its own as just a printed book. But ALL Bibles have *living words* inside them. There is a supernatural transfer happening from The Author to the reader. The same happens with our books as well because we are

Kingdom Scribes. This is no small calling. People's lives are radically changed from what we write, whether it be fiction or nonfiction.

The woman dealing with the issue of blood reached out, merely touching the hem of Jesus' garment. She was instantly healed. She didn't touch him, but only an article of his clothing. It was not even a large handful of his outfit, just a hem on the edge of his garment. No one prayed over her. No one pointed her out and called her to Jesus. She just believed in her heart that if she could just touch his clothes, then she would be set free. Wow!

Are we not praying before, during, and after we write our books? Isn't it our hope that our words would touch lives in Jesus name? Of course. Why shouldn't we expect people to be healed, delivered, and set free when they read our books? Please, don't discount your words! Your story will NEVER be just some simple tale that entertains or educates.

Believe that God has called you to release something supernatural through your writing because it is true. You are writing to heal people and set them free. The Holy Spirit will infiltrate the craziest of places in other people through your writing.

One of the prophetic words spoken over me before I started writing my first book, was that there would be a medicinal element to my writing. At the time it didn't make sense, but now, oh, I believe it!

I was contacted by an amazing woman named Liza. Here is what she wrote to me:

"Hi, Brae. It's Liza. I just want to let you know that you are helping me persevere through my current hyperbaric oxygen treatments. In God's perfect timing, I began reading Demons and Thieves *on Thursday, and it is helping the daily two hour treatments speed by! Your compelling storyline, dialogue, and emotion is a great distraction from my physical pain, the deep pressure of the chamber and the hood over my head as I breath-in 100% oxygen!!! I had been reading a few other books while in the chamber by authors like Shawn Bolz and Graham Cooke...and while they're great, the books didn't engage me as dramatically as yours. So, thank you for being right here with me in-the-midst of God's healing process in my life!!"*

Wow! God is supernaturally touching the lives of all those who read my books. I won't hear all the stories of how, when, and where. But I know in my heart there are signs and wonders taking place for those who read my books! I believe in a God that makes it all possible. And I believe our God is doing that with all his Kingdom Scribes.

Writers, write confidently. Write knowing you are imparting something supernaturally charged by the Holy Spirit inside of you.

What a privilege to be called a Scribe of the Kingdom.

Prayer: I pray for you right now that you understand the power that is at your fingertips. I pray that you steward your writing and become fully aware of who you are in Christ Jesus. You are a son/daughter of the Most High. He believes in you, and now it is time to believe the one who believes in you. It is time for you to answer your calling. Don't give up. Don't give in. Instead, rise up and go deeper into Him.

Action: Writing prompt. I want you to take the scene of the woman with the issue of blood touching the hem of Jesus' robe and write about it. I want you to bring the scene to life. Add in color, what she sees, the taste in her mouth, the emotion of the situation, the expectation, the hope she had, the touch, and what it felt like. I want you to add in all the senses and emotions. It is this type of element of writing that will supernaturally train you to write in such a way to impart healing and breakthrough for others as they read your work.

CHAPTER 25
WRITE IN A BOOK

Jeremiah 30:2 (NIV) This is what the Lord, the God of Israel, says: 'Write in a book all the words I have spoken to you.

GOD DIDN'T WRITE as a hobby, and neither should we. He is very clear to those called to write as we see in this piece of scripture. If you don't know where to start in your writing, then I would start by writing ALL the words spoken to you by God. Write out the dreams you have had, awards you received in school for writing. Write the history of your family and study if there are any writing endeavors within your heritage. Write about where you grew up and research the history of your town. Write out the prophetic words spoken over you. You might uncover something.

Now, for those of you who do not know what I mean when I say 'prophetic word,' let me explain.

Some have the gift of prophecy as we see in 1 Corinthians 14. People, in essence, can hear from the Lord and impart what they hear to an individual. It can be general, or extremely detailed, but it will always be uplifting and encouraging to the one receiving the word. Prophecy is there to edify the body of Christ.

Prophecy is a gift. The office of a Prophet is a different subject altogether, and there are plenty of books out there talking about the difference between the two if you care to dig a little deeper into the subject. I won't tackle it here.

At this point, you believe you are called to be a writer. You believe that God specifically wants you to write something and release it to the world. Some of you don't know where to start. You have no idea of how to structure your story, or even the heart of the story has not manifested yet. You might even have subtle ideas but nothing that truly hits home.

In this chapter and specifically with this scripture, you can start here and do exactly as God instructed. Write ALL the words He has spoken to you. You might already have a lot of it in journals. It is time to dig through them, compile them, get them all in one place for you to see together. Somewhere within those words is a theme, a storyline, that God will unveil.

I once heard that our tears point to our destiny. Perhaps in your journaling where you are sharing your heart, your pains, your struggles, your tears, you will find the theme that God is highlighting for your writing assignment. Maybe God wants you to blog about it and not write a book. Perhaps it is a screenplay or what about a play for Broadway. Explore with Papa God. He will direct your path. Once you lock down what it is you are supposed to write, you will eventually look back at this time you spent with God and find that you were closest with Him during the discovery. Sometimes, our writing assignment is to draw us closer to Him. Isn't that where we want to be?

Prayer: Draw us closer to you, God. We want to be with you. We want to feel you close by. As much as we want to fulfill our calling, we want to be as close to you as possible. You are inside of us. You have chosen to dwell within us. Let us not close the door but instead open it. Opening the door is an invitation to come in. To go deeper. Let us go deeper together in whatever that looks like. We are all in. Let nothing shake us. Let nothing separate us. Not even our assignment.

Action: Write out all of your prophetic words, dreams, history of your family, the history of the town you grew up in, awards you won in school, etc. Compile it all and pray into it to find what God is saying to you.

CHAPTER 26
PROPHETIC WORDS

1 Corinthians 13:9-10 (NIV) For we know in part and we prophesy in part, but when completeness comes, what is in part disappears.

PROPHETIC WORDS WE receive are very interesting. We must pray into them. But we must also understand that what people have imparted is only in part. They didn't get the complete picture, but it is our job as the recipient to press in. As the believer who received that prophecy, we must ask, seek, knock, and pray to God for clarity of the word. It might take years to fully understand the word before it is revealed. And sometimes the 'completeness' comes the next day. Remember, it is in God's perfect timing. We can rush into things, then scratch our head afterward saying, "God, what happened? I thought you said…" I've done it, we've all done it. But as we mature and grow in our faith, we start stepping into deeper wisdom. I have words that were spoken over me and have not come to pass yet. But I don't give them up. I keep reminding God that I care about fulfilling them. And, to be honest, I'm reminding myself about them too. Some words are still in process.

Let me give you my testimony with a prophetic word I received. My first book was something I had been working on for over 20 years, The Orb of Truth. It was an on-again-off-again relationship with several breakups, hitting walls all along the way. It truly has been quite a journey. It was in late 2010 when I heard clearly (and personally) from God that "we" would be finishing my book in 2011. November was when I heard this. We had been attending Awakening Church a while, and there had never been any moment of writers being pinpointed during a service. Well, a month later, all writers were called to the front of church one night. Pastor Karlet Muster prayed over each one of us, and I was given the following:

1. **Jesus would be there when I write**

2. **First of many books to write**

3. **Breakthru from writer's block**

4. **God will show me things that I would have never thought of**

5. **There would be a medicinal element to my writing**

Now, Pastor Karlet had no idea that I was a writer, or what I was writing. I had just heard from God weeks earlier that in 2011, we would finish my book. Everything was lining up.

January kicked off, and I started writing the first chapter. I had elements ready for each of my chapters, but when you co-labor with God, he will direct your path. I had my ideas but so did God. We worked together. He loved my ideas, and I cherished His input. Everything seemed to shift within my life, and I had a deeper focus. The words seemed to just flow out, with no worries over what I was going to write next or how the chapter would end. My goal was to just write and have fun! I wrote with a new confidence.

God was with me.

January 10th came along, and I was suddenly laid off from work. It was a big SHOCKER as I had been at the company for over 10 years, and then it was suddenly all over. My heart got stuck on WOW for a moment. But overall, I had a sense of peace about it, and all I could think about was writing my next chapter in my book. Don't get me wrong, I did think about providing for my family. But my wife and I had strategized together before this ever happened (you know, the 'what if you lost your job?' scenario). God is good, let's just leave it at that.

Tons of God stories came about from all of this.

I completed my first novel in six months, ran it through a critique group, hired the editor, and hired the graphic artist to do the book cover. Then, I researched how to be published, contacted publishers and, getting rejection letters, researched self-publishing.

And then it happened.

On November 12th, 2012, my first book, *The Orb of Truth*, was released.

Every one of my prophetic words happened, even the "medicinal element." I am starting to hear from people how it has healed their heart, restored hope, and more.

Prayer: Lord Jesus, I pray for a supernatural encounter for those reading this book. Speak to them through someone. Give them an encouraging word, a prophetic word, a word of knowledge. Let them hear from you directly through someone else. All glory to you, God. Your sheep hear your voice, and right now, I ask that we have ears to hear you and eyes to see what you are doing. Let a complete stranger speak something that no one would know except for you. We give you permission to give us a radical supernatural encounter. Give us a hug, Lord Jesus.

Action: Write out the prophetic words you have received. Pray over them. Memorize them. Remind God (and yourself) about them. If you have not received a prophetic word and this is something new to you as a believer, then I encourage you to look into it. Pray for God to bring you a word of encouragement and watch what happens.

SECTION FIVE
WRITER'S PARABLES
AND OTHER INSIGHTS

124

CHAPTER 27
EVERY STORY NEEDS AN EDITOR

John 15:1-2 (NIV) I am the true vine, and my Father is the gardener. He cuts off every branch in me that bears no fruit, while every branch that does bear fruit he prunes so that it will be even more fruitful.

YOUR STORY NEEDS an editor.

If God is editing us to make us better, then don't you think you also need an editor for your work?

The answer is yes.

We all need an editor before our manuscript is submitted for publication. If you are self-publishing, then you need to hire a professional editor, almost *more* than a book traditionally published. It must be a *professional* editor, not your friend, not your mom, but a professional. Let me say it again--HIRE A PROFESSIONAL.

Editing will be your biggest cost, but it will also make or break your work. I have put down numerous books because of the book's atrocious editing (or lack of editing). I can write a fantastic story, but I still need to have an editor come in and polish or sharpen things where they need to be. God cuts off every branch in us that bears no fruit, and he does this so that we will be even more fruitful. This is exactly what an editor does to your work. They are supposed to help you cut out all the bad writing so that it will be even more impactful than before. Editors have a holy mantle, a mantle they don't take for granted and nor should we. Even in the world, the editor makes life-changing choices over the written word of Scribes. Meaning, God is okay being edited by the editor. Something you might have worked on together could be challenged by your editor. Don't pull out the God card and say, "God told me specifically to say this." Once you pull out the God card then it ends all conversation. Instead, pray into it. Pray for your editor, even if you aren't working with them yet. Start praying for your editor now for your future collaboration together for your project.

Here is my own interpretation of this verse from the writer/editor perspective:

"I am the writer, and my editor is the gardener. The editor cuts off every word I write that bears no fruit, while every word that does bear fruit she sharpens so that it will be even more fruitful."

Here are two parables that God brought to me about this subject:

THE GARDENERS

There were two men growing vineyards, each in his own lot. One saw his vineyard as a masterpiece without blemish, because he loved how the vines kept growing in all directions. The other hired a gardener to come and prune back the vines not bearing fruit and help with the harvest for those vines that were.

They both opened for business. The first man realized that no one was showing up to his vineyard, although he had done, in his eyes, just as much work has his neighbor. He watched, as people from all over came to see his neighbor's vineyard. Meanwhile, none came to his. Everyone left joyful and well pleased, and the few and far between that came to his vineyard left with disappointed faces.

Interpretation: Both men wrote a book. One saw his story as incredible on its own merit. The other author went and hired an editor to come alongside and help him make his book the best it could be. Both men released their books into the world. The one who didn't hire an editor had little, if any, sales and those he did sell, left bad reviews.

The other, who hired an editor, saw a great reward. And those who came and bought his book experienced a story that touched them deeply.

THE LOST STORY AND THE BARBER

There was a man drawn into the wilderness. He was there a great many years. When he returned, no one recognized him. His hair was long, tangled, and a mess. His beard was long and without form.

It was only when he walked into the barbershop and gave his last and only coin that his identity was revealed.

He was the lost Prince of the Kingdom.

Interpretation: The man represented a book, a story yet untold. It was raw, real, and wild. When the story was revealed, no one knew its meaning for it too was raw, real, and wild. Once it was viewed by a professional with skill and their services paid for, the story was then edited to reveal the truth of the identity within its pages.

Everyone then recognized the authority that the story carried.

Prayer: We thank you, God, for editing our lives. For trimming and pruning the things in our life that are not needed for our story to grow and blossom. Thank you for taking care of us, for always being there, and for always loving us. I pray right now in Jesus name that our writings would glorify you and not ourselves. I pray that you would edit the parts that need to be pulled out in order to set our story free. We give you permission to pull the weeds out from our story. We trust you, God. We believe in you, God. We love you, God. We pray that our writing assignments glorify you and that they are an extension of our worship toward you. You deserve the glory. I pray this in Jesus mighty name. Amen.

Action: For those of you who haven't experienced an editor or the process, then I suggest as an action item to take the first chapter of your book and submit that chapter to three different editors. Basically, you are interviewing editors to see which one you like. It is a great process to discover the process of an editor and the way you will work with an editor. Remember, you are the CEO, and you are hiring an employee. You ultimately decide what you want to edit in your book. The editor is giving you suggestions, and you take those suggestions, pray over it, and then make the necessary changes to enhance the chapter.

Email three editors and ask them to edit your first chapter to see how they work. They might ask for your first five pages double-spaced dependent on how long your first chapter is. They do have a limit on what they will edit for free so just send them what they need and go from there.

First, this will give you some insight into you seeing firsthand how your work holds up to editing. Second, for those who haven't shared their work to anyone, this will open you up in ways you never could have imagined. Have fun and enjoy the process.

CHAPTER 28
INVESTIGATE EVERYTHING

Luke 1:3 (NASB) it seemed fitting for me as well, having investigated everything carefully from the beginning, to write it out for you in consecutive order, most excellent Theophilus;

RESEARCH IS CRUCIAL when writing a book. Whether it is nonfiction or fiction, you must devote time to investigate everything revolving around what you will be writing about. What other books are out there on the same subject? Has it been studied in depth? Who is the leading mind on that subject? Is what you are making up based on something well studied? Sometimes, a simple search on the internet just won't cut it. Investigate your subject thoroughly on as many avenues as possible.

When I was tackling my historical fiction, *Demons & Thieves*, I had to do massive research about the two thieves on the cross, along with the demon named Legion. Having never done Historical Fiction before, I made sure I studied the scriptures, poured over many variations, and searched the internet. All of which led me down many trails. I looked up books written about them and read several of them. And all the while, I took notes, lots of notes. I researched the timeline of Jesus' ministry and reviewed the landscape of the areas I would be writing within. It was worth it, as I wanted to keep them as accurate as possible. I'm glad I did that legwork because it all paid off. Reviews keep coming in on the accuracy of the novel. Even though I had to fictionalize quite a bit, I'm pleased with the results, and my readers are too.

We need to scrutinize what we are writing about. Everything should be carefully reviewed, from beginning to end, in order to produce something excellent for the world. Kingdom excellence doesn't mean perfection. It means that we have done our due diligence to craft the best story possible. Our excellence leaves more room for God to intervene with His divinity and make our words come alive.

The other piece about this scripture is, "**write it out for you in consecutive order.**"

I typically like to outline my books. This means I lay out what I want to accomplish in chapter one all the way to the end. Now, as I begin to write the book, some of the chapters extend to multiple chapters or a couple of chapters are combined. I do my best to figure out the direction I want to go in for that chapter. Realize that the Holy Spirit is co-laboring with you and will take out and add to what you have. Go with Him. Have fun exploring with God. He will show you things and give you ideas you never could have imagined. There are times that I have physically put up my hand to give God a high-five.

Some of you like to be a "panster" (writing by the seat of your pants). If it works for you, then go with it. If it produces fruit then who am I to judge the style that works for you. Doctor Luke apparently likes to outline his writings, and I find most writers do as well. We don't hem ourselves in with our outlines, and we will deviate as needed, but it gives us good anchor points to stay on message with our writing.

I encourage you to try it out. I personally use an excel spreadsheet and list out chapters with the name of each chapter, how many words in that chapter, and how many double-spaced pages, along with the date it was completed on. In this spreadsheet, I also keep track of the second rewrite with the same information so I can see how many words and pages changed and the date I changed it. A simple but effective way to monitor your progress. I keep adding to this spreadsheet for third rewrites and also editor rewrites. You can keep track of your beta readers, critique information, and more.

Oh, and for those wondering what I use to write in. Simple. Word document. I keep all my chapters separate, and it's own file name. I can edit chapters easily by finding them, and it helps when working with editors.

Prayer: Lord, you ask that we stay in step with you. Help us to map out our writing assignment has your Kingdom Scribe. Help us to keep things in order and give us revelation as we investigate and research what is needed. What a privilege and honor to write with you and for you. We are so thankful for the process of writing because we spend time with you. Bless our writing endeavors. Open us up to deeper truths as we research and plan it all out. Take us to depths we never thought of. To depths unseen. Reveal to us the mysteries of who you are and allow us to impart our findings in our writings. Help us to weave those mysteries into the story. You are our role model. You are our friend. You are our God. Amen!

Action: Start an excel spreadsheet or some way to keep track of your writings. If you need to handwrite into a journal, then so be it.

Chapter number, the title of chapter, words, pages, date.

Have your writings in a word document. Keep each chapter a separate file with chapter number and name of chapter to find it easily. When you do rewrites, then you save as and make a new file name saying the chapter number, name, and then v2 to represent version two.

Keep your writing in order. You can also have a spreadsheet for information about your characters, equipment, likes, dislikes, scars, dreams, and so on. Create tabs for each character. This is a resource for you to go back to as you write your story. You can also have information about cities, landscapes, flora, and fauna, etc.

I also suggest you email your chapters to yourself as a backup. Put your chapters on a thumb drive as a backup. Save your work in the cloud, such as Google Drive, as a backup. I actually work off of Google Drive for all my work now so it is automatically in the cloud and I can work anywhere in the world on any computer by logging in to my account.

The message here is to have your work backed up in multiple areas. You don't want to lose anything.

CHAPTER 29
LOST AND FOUND

Psalm 119:59 (TPT) When I realize that I'm going astray, I turn back to obey your instructions.
Psalm 119:59 (MSG) When I took a long, careful look at your ways, I got my feet back on the trail you blazed.

I T'S TIME TO take an inventory.

Many businesses do a yearly inventory. They take account of what they have and what was forgotten. It's time to make decisions about whether to keep something or throw it away. It's time to rediscover what was hidden or lost. They write off the discrepancies as a loss. And sometimes they resurrect something forgotten in the recesses of the warehouse which turns out to be a bestseller for their company. The item wasn't in the right season before, but now it is.

What is it we know, and what is it that we have forgotten or lost?

Every six months to a year, I will take an inventory of my writings. I will go through old notes, old journals, blog postings, interviews that I've written out, even sermons, and so on. When you do this, the Holy Spirit will highlight things that you might have forgotten. It is those nudges that I take notice of and then dig deeper into it through prayer, fasting, reading the Word, and resting on it.

I encourage you to look through your writings that you discounted and set aside for whatever reason. God has perfect timing for things and what was lost before or set aside because it didn't feel right back then can be a spark today. It could be as simple as a title of a book you had or the first sentence of a chapter that never took off, but suddenly a new thought arises, a new flame ignites, a new story erupts.

It's not magic, it's God.

Sometimes we can feel lost and without direction even amongst our success. *What are you talking about, Brae?* I'm talking about people can feel alone even at Church. I'm talking about a successful writer who can still feel alone in his current writing. He can be in a place of redundancy, without direction, without motivation, where writing just becomes writing. It can happen, and it can happen to us. We need to be aware of it.

Going back to your older writings can ignite the passion for writing once again. God will speak to us, encourage us, and light a fire in us we never thought possible.

I want you to always have the passion as a Kingdom Writer, a passion never extinguished. It's a HOLY PASSION like when you first heard your name called by God and answered Him.

It's getting your writing back to the heart of the matter and not just a job or an assignment or worst yet a task to complete. After publishing six successful books and now writing this one, my passion for writing has not subsided, but there have been times that I have recognized a shift within me that I shake off and then question later, "Wait, what was that?"

God answered me, "It's a demon called mundane."

These demons, like "mundane," will sneak up on you and won't shout out that it's a demon but instead hide and cloak itself within the world we live in. It will feel normal, not scary. It will be subtle, not forceful. If I told others about a demon named mundane they would squint their eyes, turn their head slightly, and then raise an eyebrow. You can't say these things in open circles, but I can tell you as a Kingdom Writer called by God because it will make sense to you. You will recall all the times in your writing path when you have dealt with "mundane." He is a crafty one, and he likes to get into your writings, make it dreary, slow the pace down, and subtly dismantle your flow. After a while you start resting in the allure of mundane, agreeing with him, and then finally looking at other things as more important, like Facebook.

This scripture speaks life to us. When we go astray, God is there for us. He reminds us. He loves us. He lights a fire within us, and we get back on the trail He blazed.

All this time you thought it was you. It was just a demon named "mundane" and guess what we do with demons? Guess what power and authority we have over demons? Yes, in Jesus name, we cast out demons. We send them packing.

Prayer: God Almighty, thank you for your authority and the authority you give to us to deal with "mundane" and the rest of his boredom outcasts. We send the demon mundane back to the Abyss in Jesus' mighty name. Lord, help us to get back on track with you and the assignment we have been given by you. Writing for you and to you is such an honor. We cherish our writing time because we are close to you. Let nothing come between us. Nothing the enemy sends will prevent us from being in your Presence. It's your Presence that matters most above and beyond the actual writing and yet the writing you love for us to do. You are the most incredible God. You are worthy of it all, and we thank you. We love you. We worship you. We praise you. All in Jesus name. Amen!

Action #1: Find a quiet place where no one can hear you. Place one hand on your heart, and the other hand on your head. Say out loud to yourself:

"I pledge to take full inventory

of what you have placed inside of me.

Known and unknown.

Thank you God for all you have provided,

all that you have deposited,

all that you have developed,

and all that you are developing inside of me.

In this season, as I take a long, careful look at your ways,

place my feet on the trail

and ignite my heart to step into places

I never thought possible.

Take my weaknesses and make them strong.

I trust you.

Now let me have the faith to walk that trust out with you.

Hallelujah!!!

Action Step #2: Sit down, close your eyes, and listen. Write down what you hear the Holy Spirit imparting to you. If you don't hear anything, then repeat the above saying it out loud again and then sit and listen. Continue until you start hearing something.

God speaks to his people.

CHAPTER 30
TWO BY TWO

Mark 6:7 (NIV) Calling the Twelve to him, he began to send them out two by two and gave them authority over impure spirits.

JESUS NEVER SENT his disciples out alone.

There is something powerful in this scripture for us writers. I think it is very important that we don't isolate but instead find people to gather with. Jesus sent them out two by two, and I believe we should find someone to go out and write with, following Jesus' example. Yes, you will write individually, but there is something supernatural to having someone at the same table writing what they are called to write while you write yours.

I liken it the same as finding a workout partner. You workout individually, but you go together. Why? You encourage one another. You create a spark to work harder, and you also find enjoyment in the relationship. The same is true for writing. Find your writing partner or partners and go and write together. How awesome for you and your writing partner(s) to say you were in battle together, bringing about the stories from Heaven's vault.

Look again at the last part of this chapter's scripture. Jesus gave them authority over impure spirits.

Say what?

Does this mean that as you go out to write together that you will gain authority over impure spirits who want to infiltrate your writing?

I believe so. Remember, writing should not be treated as a hobby. It is your calling. Take into account all that you do, perceive, and express. You will begin to read scripture in a new light as you step into your calling. What once meant one thing to you in a previous season now means something different.

Are they both correct? Yes.

While tapping away at your keyboard, weaving your words together to express the tale, it is then that the enemy slips in under the radar and infiltrates your assignment. It happens as your write. A simple distraction. A choppy transition. Pride. It is then that unclean spirits assault you. You will notice it when you hit a spot where you need to transition. Your flow becomes choppy like a sudden storm rose up against you. You will settle back in, but deep down, you reflect on what happened. When you come back around for rewrites and editing you will see the disrupted flow.

It's subtle. So I come back to this scripture, I pray into it, and then realized this applies to writers as well. We can get together. Two or more. God is with us, and God has also given us authority over impure thoughts. Impure suggestions. Disruptions. Little foxes coming into our garden, our story, and disrupting the flow.

Get with someone who writes. Set up a time once a week and get together. You don't need to sit and talk, just sit and write side by side. You can test it out. Write alone, which most of us do, but then write with someone at your local coffee shop or anywhere you choose and see what happens.

God's Word is life, and the depth of understanding it is something no one can fully appreciate. I believe we will be learning about the awesomeness of God for all eternity.

Prayer: We thank you, God, for giving us authority over impure spirits. Help us, teach us, how to cast these "thought-stealers" away in Jesus name. Guide us as we get together as Kingdom Writers to tell the tales you want released into the world. Guide our work to be holy before you. You are the author and finisher of our faith. We put our trust in you, God, and nobody else. Thank you for empowering us. Thank you for showing us the way. Amen.

Action: Find a writing partner and set up a consistent time to meet each week to write together. Meet up at a local coffee shop, your home, a restaurant, or whatever works for you both to have space to write. Remember, this is not a complete social hangout. Yes, please talk to one another but also fit in time to write. Share your work with one another, encourage each other, and walk out your calling together.

CHAPTER 31
GET IT OUT

Deuteronomy 31:24 (NASB) It came about, when Moses finished writing the words of this law in a book until they were complete,

ON'T EDIT, DON'T rewrite, just write.

This is something I say all the time to writers. You need to schedule your time and write it all out until it is done. You can refer back to chapter 27 in regards to the editing process, but in this chapter, we are focusing on getting your story out of your head and onto paper.

You need to vomit the book out of you. Get it onto paper, onto the computer, just get it out. Afterward, you then go back to do rewrites.

Time and time again, I hear writers struggling with the first chapter because they just can't stop trying to make it perfect. It is too easy to get caught up with editing it over and over. This rewriting and rewriting stresses a writer out because their first chapter is just never perfect enough. They get caught up in perfection. Soon after, the project just becomes too much or too overwhelming to continue.

If you can just write and get the words out of you, then you can complete your book. No one is going to read it in its raw state, so stop letting that lie of perfection slow you down.

I recall seeing a cartoon floating around social media. It was a doctor's office. The doctor was talking to the patient who was sitting down and looking up at an x-ray of his chest. The doctor is telling the man, "I believe you have a book inside of you."

How prophetic that image is for most of us. We do have a book inside of us. The doctor, representing God, can see it there, you know its there, and now it is time to get that book out of there. It does no good inside of you, and over time it will end up damaging you. I have spoken on this in other chapters.

One of the most freeing things that I impart to you is to just let it out. Don't think and ponder every word but instead, just get into a flow with the Holy Spirit. Once you get it all out, then you can go back and do the rewrites. Just getting it out will make you feel so much better. A huge sigh of relief will hit you.

I have had so many people come to me and just say, "Thank you." I ask why, and they proceed to explain how I freed them up to just write and not think about all the details of sentence structure, run-on sentences, grammar, etc. They just began to write and push to get it out of their system.

I think the gestation of a baby in the womb is a good model to go by for writers. We can write a book in nine months. Some can do it in six, and others do it in twelve, but on average you can do nine. This means you have to write. You have to have the baby in nine months. I didn't say publish it, I said, write the first draft of your book or screenplay in nine months.

Get it out! That book, story, blog, magazine, screenplay, spoken word, poem, inside of you wants to be let out. It's time to answer that call.

Prayer: Papa God, help us to get that book, that is penned up inside of us, out. Give us the tools to provoke us to let it out. Help us to not judge our work, to not edit it, but to simply let it out. Our heart's desire is to produce what you have called us to do. Help us to navigate the steps needed to do that. We trust you, and we thank you for believing in us. Amen.

Action: Write your second chapter first and then go back to the first chapter. I know it is strange, but I think it will break something off of you. I think it will allow you to have breakthrough in your 'continuous' flow of writing. The second chapter can be the hardest for those who need to have the first part perfect. Many never even get to the second chapter because they are stuck on the first. Let's hurdle the first chapter for now (even if you have already started it) and write the next one.

For those of you who are beyond the first chapter and have hit a roadblock then I suggest writing a chapter that you have imagined writing and really want to get to it. Skip everything and go to that chapter that is on your heart to write and go for it. This will free things up for you, and then you can go back to fill in the gaps.

CHAPTER 32
BOAST THE NAME OF THE LORD

Psalm 20:7 (NASB) Some boast in chariots and some in horses,
But we will boast in the name of the Lord, our God.

OUR BOASTING, OUR trusting, our affections, need to be on God, not on the things of this world.

Oh, how true this is. The world we live in looks to only what is in front of them. The world looks at the things we own, those things that have a finite life, and think of their future as only a dream. We have all been there. And even now some reading this will agree that they are still there. Scripture tells us to think of heavenly things and stay anchored behind the veil. As Kingdom citizens, we are here to boast about God and all that He has done and all that He is doing.

When it comes to our writing, we need to be thinking about the generations coming after us, not the here and now. Do you realize that your stories will endure through the ages? Do you realize others will pick up where you left off and build upon the revelation you received from God?

It is sometimes difficult to imagine not being in this world. Take a moment and consider it. We will be in heaven, a place foreign to our mind but familiar to our heart. We are not there yet. We were destined for this time, this place, even the family you were assigned to. And all of your experiences, good and bad, can be used to boast the name of the Lord, our God, loudly to this fallen world full of people chasing down chariots and horses.

It's okay to have nice things. That is not the issue. The issue is when our focus is solely on those nice things--focusing on the creation and not the Creator. It's a habit to break, like any other. It's a muscle that needs no starving. Our longings should be for Christ Jesus, not a new car or pony. That was our former life. We are a new creation.

Let's tell the world through our writing about the glorious place beyond this world that we are destined for. Let's set people free through our stories so they can stop boasting about themselves and instead boast about their Creator.

Our writings will go further than we can. As a Kingdom Writer, this is our superpower. Long after we are gone, back to our home in heaven, our books will continue to be read and enjoyed. Imagine your books reaching kings and queens around the world, Muslims, Hindus, all cultures, races, and religions, the homosexual community, and the President of the United States. It's happening. Everyone I mentioned above is reading, and one day your book might end up in their hands. One day the words you wrote with the love of Christ will be imparted to someone reading your book and be forever changed.

One day will only come when you sit and write what you are called to write.

Prayer: Lord, I pray for discernment. Give us discernment in always boasting about you and not of ourselves. Help us to keep our tongue in obedience when we are at a social gathering. Let us not boast about fame but instead use our fame to boast about you. We thank you for the open doors that are coming but give us discernment on which doors to walk through and which doors to close. Some of the doors are not meant for us to go through, so we ask for wisdom in knowing. Lead us. Protect us. We ask this humbly in Jesus name. Amen.

Action: Writing prompt: Write a story about someone (a person mentioned above, whether it be a king or a Muslim, etc.) that finds your book, reads it, and discovers the truth of who God is. This prompt can be changed up a bit to be your blog, or your magazine, or your screenplay. The goal is for you to see how your story impacts a person and a culture long after you are gone. Give us the emotions of this person reading. Give us their questions and answer God gives them while reading. Give us the struggle of the person reading truth. Let the Holy Spirit guide you as you write this encounter out.

CHAPTER 33
THE GENERATIONS NEED US

Psalm 78:1-4 (MSG) Listen, dear friends, to God's truth,
bend your ears to what I tell you.
I'm chewing on the morsel of a proverb;
I'll let you in on the sweet old truths,
Stories we heard from our fathers,
counsel we learned at our mother's knee.
We're not keeping this to ourselves,
we're passing it along to the next generation—
God's fame and fortune,
the marvelous things he has done.

D O WE NOT share stories that are very similar but told in a different voice or from a different angle?
Yes, because they are tried and true.

I love the Message version of this psalm. It is packed with so much goodness for us writers. It truly speaks for itself. The Holy Spirit is already revealing things to you as you read it, so read it over and over. I pray right now that you have ears to hear what He is saying to you and eyes to see what He is showing you.

"Listen, dear friends, to God's truth."

The psalmist states that he is "chewing" on a tale. He is receiving some great revelation from an old story of the past—one that everyone had heard before. I love the ending of the psalm as it changes to a generational mindset. No longer are we to keep things to ourselves in this time and place. We can't be worried or striving for worldly success for our lifetime. We must realize that we are affecting generations coming. We are Kingdom Writers to change the future. And while some of us will generate worldly fame and fortune, that shouldn't be the scribal ambition. We will generate fame and fortune, just not for us.

It is ALL for God. He is the famous one.

We cannot be Kingdom Writers if it is all about us and our own success. If that is the direction you want to go in, then you are a writer who happens to be a Christian. But for those called (and I mean called), then you are embarking on a holy journey. It's all about what matters to our King and representing His kingdom well to bring Him glory and honor.

Your book could only sell one copy. But that copy could bring the moment that God speaks powerfully to that reader. Then that single reader could end up becoming the next CS Lewis or JRR Tolkien or the next Billy Graham or President that reaches millions. Your book may not be read until long after you are dead, and then someone may find it on accident (they think). Only then can your seed bear its intended fruit. Your words may then have become "sweet old truths" that reach millions. Are you ready to be that kind of writer? That Kingdom scribe?

Do what you are called to do. And do your best. Then let God do what He always had destined to do through your written works. The generations need your writings!

Fathers and mothers will be telling our tales to their children. You will be part of the next generation as your work infiltrates hearts and minds. God will work powerfully through your writings to reach people He destined to read your work before time ever began. It truly blows my mind when you start delving into the depths of God. A depth that no one can ever reach the bottom.

We are passing along God's fame and fortune, which is the marvelous things He has done. We will be releasing testimonies of miracles, and those reading will end up receiving a miracle themselves. It's the power of a testimony, which means 'do it again.'

What about the fiction stories that will cut through hardened hearts and allow the Holy Spirit to break in and set them free. This is happening today with written works, and it will continue to happen. When you release your work out into the world, know that God has plans with it and with you. It's a supernatural process, and through the hard work of our writing assignments, we can at times see the fruit and taste to see it is good.

Prayer: I bless your writing in the name of Jesus to affect generations to come. You are a Kingdom Writer destined to awaken others who read your work. Your writing is anointed. Your writing will heal people, set captives free, and ultimately nudge the reader's hearts open enough for God to infiltrate and introduce the love He has for them. I pray that you write with joy and impart joy through your writings in Jesus mighty name.

Action: Write a story that your mother or father told you as a child. Remind yourself how these stories they told you have affected you today. If it wasn't them who told you a story, then write about a particular story that comes to your mind from your childhood. Write it in your journal.

CHAPTER 34
MAKE TIME, NOT EXCUSES

Proverbs 21:5 (ESV) The plans of the diligent lead surely to abundance, but everyone who is hasty comes only to poverty.

MAKE TIME, NOT excuses.

Is it better to say, "I'm too busy for the King," or, "I'm too busy with the King?"

Most, if not all, published authors have had to come out of something before going into writing full-time. In all the interviews, you will either hear or read about, there is hardly ever anyone saying anything about how they didn't have enough time. They made time instead of excuses. They cut non-essentials out of their lives and made writing a priority.

My friend, Paul Young, author of *The Shack*, wrote his book on the train to and from work. And he was working three jobs. I wrote *Demons & Thieves* while working full-time, running Kingdom Writers Association, spending time with my wife, loving on my grandchildren, being a Pastor at our church, preaching, teaching, traveling, etc. I never compromised having fun with friends and family, but I committed myself to spend time writing at least an hour a day.

It is possible if you let God do the impossible.

Do you know that the average person watches up to 5 hours of television per day? Even if you only watch an hour a day, you can trade it in. There is your writing time. Bingo. Now, the question is, what are you going to decide? You can perfect your excuses all day long, but that book inside of you will remain forever entombed within you.

The scripture above talks about the plans of the diligent person leading to abundance. This abundance it speaks of is the fullness of joy and strength for mind, body, and soul. That is incredible. As a Kingdom Writer, you can tap into this abundance that God speaks of. Or you can be hasty, or looking for the easy way out, and only find poverty. This poverty does not come from coins missing from your pocket or money in your bank. No, this poverty is in your spirit. You will feel incomplete, not full of joy in your heart. Something will be missing. That is the poverty it speaks of. Don't let excuses get in the way. Make time for this calling you have received.

My friend, Lynn Vincent, author of *Heaven Is For Real* and *Same Kind of Different As Me*, said it best at our Kingdom Creativity Conference, "Put your butt in the chair and write."

Prayer: I know it is not easy, Lord, but we thank you for this calling you have placed upon us. I pray that we rise up to the challenge. Help us navigate our own excuses for not obeying the call you have placed upon us. Help us to say no to things that would interfere with our time with you to write. Give us a hunger to be with you and write with you. Give us an insatiable thirst to scribe our story. Help us to set aside the necessary time to get our project done. We ask this in Jesus name. Amen.

Action: Place post-it notes around the house, giving yourself encouraging messages to write. Encourage yourself with messages that say 'you can do this' and 'never give up.'

Put your butt in the chair and write.

CHAPTER 35
A DEAD MAN CAN'T WRITE

Romans 6: 8-11 (NIV) Now if we died with Christ, we believe that we will also live with him. For we know that since Christ was raised from the dead, he cannot die again; death no longer has mastery over him. The death he died, he died to sin once for all; but the life he lives, he lives to God. In the same way, count yourselves dead to sin but alive to God in Christ Jesus.

A DEAD MAN CAN'T write, or can he?

There are two sides to my thoughts on the previous statement. One is from the viewpoint of a lost soul in this world with no direction, no purpose, no hope. They have a calling on their life that is lost to them for whatever circumstances happened to them as a child, an adult, or somewhere in between. They are, in essence, "the walking dead." They are going through the motions, punching a time clock each step of their lives with a soulless look on their faces. God is knocking at the door of their heart, but for whatever reason they are stuck, ignore the call on their life, ignore the whispers of God, are caught up in the cogs of this world.

Now, the other side of this is where the scripture comes in. We were once "the walking dead," but now are alive in Christ. Our sin chained us to death, but Jesus broke the chains and set us free. We died with Christ and are now alive with Christ. We are "the resurrected dead." There is an awakening inside of us. Living water flows from within. The scales from our eyes that once saw the gray matter of the world is now full of color, vibrant, alive, and thirsty for our destiny.

When we write, we write from a different perspective, a Kingdom perspective. We now have the unique ability to go to any level of the world(s) and pull from it to write as instructed by the Holy Spirit. We can write from the perspective of Hell, and we can write from the perspective of Heaven.

And we can write from any perspective in between.

We are anchored in Jesus. We are His scribes, reporting on what we see. We can be reporters sharing the facts, and we can be storytellers weaving the truth into fictional tales. And we can mix the two together. We can be all things because we are now fully alive in Christ. Our writing is alive. Our stories are alive. Our words are like fireworks to the soul. We spark others who read our works to life. We will see people healed and delivered from our writings. Why? Because we are dead to ourselves and alive in Christ. He lives within us. We cannot fail if we press in. We are victorious as we walk our lives out with Him.

Do you remember walking in the shadow of your destiny? You know, that feeling that you are just missing something but you shrug your shoulders, hunker down, work harder, and move on. Then Jesus shows up on the scene, you hear Him call your name, you answer Him, and then He shows you a whole new world. He shows us our destiny, our calling in life. He awakens the dead man walking to a live man walking.

There should be nothing standing in our way of what He has called us to do. The enemy will continue to assault us, but we take authority of those situations (Mark 16:17-18), stand our ground firm (Ephesians 6:14), and are ready in season and out of season (2 Timothy 4:2).

As a believer, we are dead. To ourselves. But we are ALIVE in Christ. It's time we start writing like we are alive in Him and stop writing like a dead man.

Prayer: Lord, I pray for the readers to be brought to the revelation of their death and life in Christ. Let them recognize your power of life inside of them and break the chains once and for all of the old man clawing his way back from the dead. Let our time here be focused on you and not the distractions of this world. Prepare us with the armor of God to stand firm against our adversary. Prepare us to be ready in season and most importantly out of season. Let us be ready at all times and in all situations. Let our writings also break the chains binding people and holding them back from their true calling. We thank you in advance of what you are doing through our writings. You are worthy of it all. Amen.

Action: Memorize these verses.

Mark 16:17-18

Ephesians 6:14

2 Timothy 4:2

CHAPTER 36
EVEN ANIMALS KNOW
THEIR CALLING

Job 12:9-12 (MSG) But ask the animals what they think—let them teach you; let the birds tell you what's going on.
Put your ear to the earth—learn the basics.
Listen—the fish in the ocean will tell you their stories.
Isn't it clear that they all know and agree that God is sovereign, that he holds all things in his hand—
Every living soul, yes, every breathing creature?
Isn't this all just common sense, as common as the sense of taste?
Do you think the elderly have a corner on wisdom, that you have to grow old before you understand life?

EVERY CREATURE KNOWS their purpose, but man doesn't (not outside of Christ, anyway).

What I feel led to say about this is that even the animals know their calling in life.

Why do we get caught up with living lives like the creatures of the earth on autopilot instead of living a life beyond survival? The animals understand their place and their function, so why don't we?

Each of us, if we truly look within, know that there is something more to life than just getting by. Discovering what that is is exhilarating and scary all at the same time. God will even use the major disruptions in our lives to provoke us toward our destiny.

I remember losing my job all of a sudden after being an exemplary employee for over a decade. A week earlier, I was pleading and crying out to God to help me write my first book—the one I had been fumbling with for the last twenty years. Then, out of nowhere, I was let go. After that 'devastation'(the loss of my job), over the next several years, I had published seven books and produced an audiobook, started Kingdom Writers Association, traveled the world, equipped and trained hundreds of other authors, and so much more. I see God's hand so clearly now. I'm so grateful for that so-called 'devastation' event in my life. God turned it to good.

I'm not saying quit your job but recognize the hand of God when trials and tribulations occur in your life. I didn't intend to have my job drop out from under my feet. I was paid well. I liked the people I worked with. I was good at what I did. But my destiny was always to be a Kingdom Writer for God. I called out to Him, and He answered my prayer.

It is time to pick up your pen and write. It's your destiny.

Prayer: I pray for you right now as a called Kingdom Writer to press into the more that God has for you. He hears your prayers. He knows your heart. And now I pray that you have ears to hear Him and eyes to see Him. I pray this in Jesus name. Amen.

Action: If you haven't written much, then just start scribbling in a journal. Do it daily. Then expand into poetry or short story. A good place to start is to tell your story or certain aspects of your life. "I remember the time…"

If you are a veteran writer, then I challenge you to go deeper into your writing.

What do I mean by that?

Well, perhaps it might be time for you to explore a new genre. I always thought I would just write epic fantasy books. But God maneuvered me to write children's picture books, historical fiction, and now a devotional. Remember, it doesn't have to be perfect. God takes care of that. Just write and get it onto paper or computer. It's the journey that you discover yourself more than the finishing of a project.

CHAPTER 37
TRUTH AND LIES

2 Corinthians 4:4 (NLT) "Satan, who is the god of this world, has blinded the minds of those who don't believe. They are unable to see the glorious light of the Good News. They don't understand this message about the glory of Christ, who is the exact likeness of God."

THE TRUTH IS so important, so valuable, that satan (little 's') made it a point to ensure it stays barricaded by lies upon lies. Look at this chapter's scripture. If you had the most valuable item in all creation locked inside of a vault, what would you do to protect it? Well, you do have the most valuable thing in all creation. It's called The Truth.

I imagine lies much like the 'agents' within the movie *The Matrix*. They protect the truth at all cost so that the people plugged into the matrix remain lied to, deceived, and continue on with their mundane meaningless lives.

God's Word is a lamp unto our feet, right? (Psalm 119:105) This scripture now becomes critical in our walk. Why? Because without God's Word, we will be deceived once again. God lights our path, He brings us into the truth, and He teaches us how to remain in truth.

Satan also knows The Truth, and he doesn't want anyone else to know. What does he do to keep it from being found? He barricades the vault that contains Truth with lies. Centuries have gone by, and every day another lie is added to the front entrance. Those lies are making it more and more difficult for anyone trying to navigate the barricade.

Now, I'm not saying satan has God hidden in a vault. Never!

Let me ask you a question. Why doesn't everyone believe in Jesus? Now read the quote again. If you didn't want someone to know the truth, then you will mislead them away. You will redirect them. If you do, you will make them want to look (or go) in the opposite direction. Now, if satan is the "deceiver," then you better believe that he has blockaded "The Truth" with an incredible amount of lies. He has been working on this since the beginning of time, and he doesn't require sleep or food. This deception is his main course of study. And he is so clever that he can even present to us truth that can lead us further from "absolute" truth. Satan will use God's Word to mislead, redirect, confuse, and so on.

We see this being done every second of every day, and I see a lot of this flooding our world through the written. A million books are released each year, and 99% are full of deception, misleadings, and redirects. Lies attempting to bury the Truth.

This is where we come into play. This is where we see the importance of our calling by God. This is where we take a stand and fight alongside our God. This is where we stop pretending and start writing. This is where we take what is inside of us seriously and start producing Kingdom fruit. This is where we declare that we are Kingdom Writers and prove it. God fights His battles with us. He allows us to get our skin in the game, and this is where we wholeheartedly say, "Yes and amen!"

Enough is enough. At some point, we need to put our foot down and say, "You will not take any more ground, satan!" This is when we lift our staff into the air like Gandalf in *Lord of the Rings*, then slam it down onto the ground, yelling, "You shall not pass!"

Now, the battle belongs to the Lord, BUT we need to show up in our armor, ready to go to war. We need to dip our quills into the ink and strike the paper like a master swordsman. There are stories to chase down into dark lairs where no mortal man would venture, but only Kingdom Writers, who know their calling in life, would be willing to traverse.

Are you one of those I speak of above? Are you one to chase down the story inside of you and have it submit to your will?

Prayer: Lord Jesus, thank you for igniting a fire inside of us. Let our tapping of keys on a keyboard or our pen on paper spark and ignite the fuel of destiny inside of those reading what we wrote. Let us pull from the passion of our relationship with you and impart it to others that take in our stories. Partner with us, Holy Spirit, to become fishers of men with our words. Teach us, Holy Spirit, to persevere the distractions of this world and the wisdom to discern the lies that Satan whispers to us. We wear our armor, ready for battle, every time we sit at our desk and write. Give us the courage to stand our ground and not be moved by the enemy. I pray this in Jesus name, amen.

Action: Write down in your journal today's date and tell yourself that you are answering the call that God has placed upon you as His Kingdom Writer. Today is the day.

After you write it down, let it be a covenant between you and God. Say out loud and in your heart that you will write every day until it is done.

Start writing your story immediately. Like, right now. Don't delay. Start writing. I want you to write a full-page and don't stop until you are done. Let that be your pace every day until your writing assignment is complete.

BRAE'S TIDBITS

CHAPTER 38
THE HERO AND THE CHRISTIAN

Most writers know about the twelve stages of "The Hero's Journey" by Joseph Campbell's book The Hero With A Thousand Faces. It is a common template for tales that involve a hero. The hero goes on an adventure and, in a decisive crisis, wins a victory, then comes home transformed.

As Christians, we can struggle with ourselves being remotely close to hero status. I mean, we are not fighting dragons or saving damsels in distress.

But aren't we?

Do we not contend against evil daily? Do we not help people in need whenever possible? Are we not involved with God's plan to reach people with the love, power, and truth of who He is? Are we not picking up our sword, the Word of Truth, training and wielding it against our enemies? Do we not have signs and wonders following us that have faith? Jesus commanded us to cast out demons, heal the sick, and set the captives free. As writers, are we not contending against demons and principalities (Ephesians 6:12) every time we sit down to write?

If that is not heroic status than what is?

I think it's time to take an(other) honest look at who and whose you are. We are victorious people, regardless of anything we do. We have inherited victory. We are grafted into victory. We are more than conquerors, which means we have not won only one victory--we have won ALL victories.

Why?

Because our identity is found in Jesus. We are in Him, and He is in us. We are sons and daughters, no longer orphans. To be a Christian is to *live* the Hero's Journey from faith to faith. Our lives have meaning and purpose. The 12 points of the Hero's Journey are a part of our faith journey.

Let's apply the Hero's Journey to our Faith Journey through the twelve stages outlined:

1. **THE ORDINARY WORLD:** Before we knew anything, we were lost inside of this ordinary world as a broken man or woman. We are unhappy and unfilled.

2. **THE CALL TO ADVENTURE:** At some point, we are introduced to God or the idea of God.

3. **REFUSAL OF THE CALL:** We go through our uncertainty of Christianity or of God. We back away from the unknown.

4. **MEETING WITH THE MENTOR:** Many of us have someone in life that encouraged us. Most likely, it was by a relative, spouse, friend, pastor, or through the urgings of (ultimately) the Holy Spirit.

5. **CROSSING THE THRESHOLD:** This is when we fall on our knees in acceptance of what Jesus accomplished through the Cross and His resurrection.

6. **TESTS, ALLIES, AND ENEMIES:** Jesus said we would face trials and tribulations. We encounter discouragement, persecution, spiritual attacks, rejection, and suffering while friends and mentors are attained (and weights and enemies are left behind) along our journey.

7. **APPROACH to the Inmost Cave:** This is where we have the discovery of internal obstacles to God. These are the big

questions inside of us that we never knew we had until we go through the fire of faith.

8. **THE ORDEAL:** We choose the disciplined life (death to self, putting God first, and trusting His ways).

9. **THE REWARD:** This is where we discover and grasp our true identity in Christ. We are SONS and DAUGHTERS of the Most High, and we will not be shaken.

10. **THE ROAD BACK:** We take our wisdom to the ordinary world we came from. The adventure has internalized the truths, we are no longer the same and don't want others to stay the same.

11. **THE RESURRECTION:** Testing doesn't stop, but now our testing also affects others around us. A great test comes that we have feared, not accounted for, or it happens to someone we love. Our trust in God is tested in a way that would have separated us before.

12. **RETURN WITH THE ELIXIR:** Our new identity and life are triumphant over the Great Test. We can now help others discover their identity in Christ.

This is a simplistic view of the twelve stages of the Hero's Journey. And, as some of us know, some of these stages repeatedly happen before we progress to the next stage. Sometimes stages are skipped altogether. But we can all come to agree that we are on the greatest adventure in our life with God. There is so much more out there for us if we would only take the time to look. The world wants to distract us from looking! But if you can push through the ordinary world, then you will see the extraordinary world that God calls us to live in.

Action: Write out your testimony as a "Hero" following the stages presented above. If any of the stages don't apply to you, then move to the next one. Have fun reminding yourself that you are truly a Hero.

CHAPTER 39
WHAT DOES GOD THINK ABOUT PUBLISHING?

According to Strong's Concordance, the word 'publish' in the Bible is the Greek word diaggello (phonetic spelling: de-ang-gel'-lo) which means 'to publish abroad, proclaim.' The definition is, 'I announce throughout the world, spread the news of, give notice of, teach.'

THE DEFINITION OF publishing also strengthens what we must do. In all formats, written and spoken, we are to announce throughout the world, spreading the good news of Jesus Christ. This entire book is devoted to scribes and writing as a Kingdom Writer.

Now, do we have to write about God in everything we do?

No.

Some of you might think my answer is blasphemous. But one of God's books in the Bible doesn't mention God at all. It also happens to house the first scripture of nine scriptures that I will present for you below.

Esther doesn't talk about God. But God is completely infused in her actions, and in the book itself.

What does that show us as writers? It shows that we can write stories that have deep implications pointing to God without talking about God. *Lord of the Rings*, *The Matrix Trilogy*, and many others have deep meaning within the story pointing to a Creator. Yet none of them are explicitly about the Creator. Those stories have reached millions and continue to be used regularly in our everyday lives (talking to people, sermons, revelatory examples in books and articles, etc.).

What does God think about publishing? Our Bible is printed. In fact, as I said before, the Bible sells 50 copies per minute and has sold over 5 billion copies. He thinks a great deal about it.

I believe God will give us strategies in strengthening the broken industry of publishing and Christian scribes will rise to the top. It is going to take time, commitment, and understanding. What we build today is what we handoff to the next generation.

Here are nine scriptures to support publishing for the Kingdom.

*Esther 4:8 NIV -He also gave him a copy of the text of the edict for their annihilation, which had been **published** in Susa, to show to Esther and explain it to her, and he told him to instruct her to go into the king's presence to beg for mercy and plead with him for her people.*

*Daniel 6:10 NIV -Now when Daniel learned that the decree had been **published**, he went home to his upstairs room where the windows opened toward Jerusalem. Three times a day he got down on his knees and prayed, giving thanks to his God, just as he had done before.*

*Daniel 6:12 NIV -So they went to the king and spoke to him about his royal decree: "Did you not **publish** a decree that during the next thirty days anyone who prays to any god or human being except to you, Your Majesty, would be thrown into the lions' den?" The king answered, "The decree stands—in accordance with the law of the Medes and Persians, which cannot be repealed."*

*Esther 1:20 ASV -And when the king's decree which he shall make shall be **published** throughout all his kingdom (for it is great), all the wives will give to their husbands honor, both to great and small.*

*Esther 3:14 ASV -A copy of the writing, that the decree should be given out in every province, was **published** unto all the peoples, that they should be ready against that day.*

*Esther 8:13 ASV -A copy of the writing, that the decree should be given out in every province, was **published** unto all the peoples, and that the Jews should be ready against that day to avenge themselves on their enemies.*

*Psalm 68:11 ASV -The Lord giveth the word: The women that **publish** the tidings are a great host.*

*Psalm 79:13 AMP -So we Your people, the sheep of Your pasture, Will give You thanks forever; We will declare and **publish** Your praise from generation to generation.*

*Jeremiah 50:2 AMP -Declare among the nations. Lift up a signal [to spread the news]—**publish** and proclaim it, Do not conceal it; say, 'Babylon has been taken, Bel [the patron god] has been shamed, Marduk (Bel) has been shattered. Babylon's images have been shamed, her [worthless] idols have been thrown down.'*

CHAPTER 40
DISCIPLINE

- *Proverbs 12:1 "Whoever loves discipline loves knowledge, but whoever hates correction is stupid."*

- *2 Timothy 1:7 "For the Spirit God gave us does not make us timid, but gives us power, love and self-discipline."*

It's like going to the gym. You need to get yourself acclimated. Discipline your mind and body to come into alignment with who you are as a writer. Let your passion for writing come alive. Get into a rhythm of writing each day. Start with a sentence. Grow into a paragraph. Hit your stride with a page a day. Each chapter will be a short story. Connect them together, and they become a book.

Short stories are the breadcrumbs that lead to great stories. If you treat each chapter like a short story and then connect them with multiple ones—look out!

Be disciplined in your craft. Take classes, go to conferences, take workshops, read a lot of good and great books. Throw in a bad book to see the difference and to know what you are steering away from as a writer yourself. We can learn from others, and we *should* learn from others.

Write daily. Set up a schedule. Be diligent.

CHAPTER 41
GOAL SETTING

- *2 Chronicles 15:7 "But as for you, be strong and do not give up, for your work will be rewarded."*

- *Proverbs 16:3 "Commit to the Lord whatever you do, and he will establish your plans."*

SET A MONTHLY goal and then set some yearly goals. Goals help us. Write down goals like this; for example, "By the end of this month I will complete chapter one of my book."

"By the end of this year, I will complete my book."

Once you write these goals down, always have them in front of you to remind you. Then you will start working on completing those goals.

Other goals can be to find a critique group, find a writers group who encourages each other, get more training, attend a writers conference or workshop, find a writing partner, or any combination of the above.

Calendar your writing time.

Protect your writing time. Don't overextend yourself with "yes." This means you have to say "no" at times that will try to interfere with your writing schedule. Perhaps it is a movie date with friends or a dinner out. I will say, though, do not sacrifice your family time or time with your husband or spouse in the name of writing your book. That is not what I'm talking about. Protect your family time first and foremost.

Cut out the TV. That is a big one. Cut out your social media time. This also bleeds into the next chapter on time management.

Over my years of writing I have a goal of completing a chapter a day when I go into writing mode. This ranges from 1,000 to 5,000 words on average per day. If it is a 30 day month then I should be able to produce a 30K to 150k word book within that time. You might be amazed at those numbers, but it is very doable. It wasn't at first, mind you. I started small and worked my little tiny writing muscles until I was able to lift heavier writing time. It has become my normal, but it wasn't my normal to begin with. Set your goals and work toward them. You can do this. I believe in you. Better yet, our God believes in you.

CHAPTER 42
TIME MANAGEMENT

- *Ephesians 5:15-16 "Be very careful, then, how you live—not as unwise but as wise, 16 making the most of every opportunity, because the days are evil."*

- *John 9:4 "As long as it is day, we must do the works of him who sent me. Night is coming, when no one can work."*

CALENDAR YOUR TIME with friends and family- get it done or your forever talking about getting it done. If I had a dollar given to me for every time I heard someone tell me they have a book they need to write, then I would be set for life.

It saddens me when I hear the heart of so many called to write, and yet they never do. There is a graveyard of stories out there, some to be resurrected, but others never to be heard because it was that person's story and no one else can tell it.

This is your time. This is your life. This is your moment. What are you going to do? Don't fall into the trap of saying you don't have the time. You do. Turning off the TV is the biggest thing. If you have a show you watch— that takes up just an hour. Turn off the TV and write for an hour instead. It comes down to prioritizing. What is important to you?

But Brae, you don't understand, I have no brain power to write after a long day. Well, you need to train yourself to break out of that. You need to dig deep to find freedom. Don't get lazy, get active. Remember, one sentence a day turns into a paragraph which turns into a page which turns into a chapter which turns into a book. You can do this.

Answer the call that God has placed upon you. Sow into it and reap your harvest all to bring Him glory. It's not about us, it is about Him.

Map out one of your weeks. Take each day and write out as you go— what you are doing, how much time it took to do that. Write the importance level of what it was you did from low, medium, and high.

The bathroom would be high. It's something I would call a "static duty." It's something you have to do. Same as eating. But what about TV? How does it rate and how much time do you do it? What about YouTube videos? What about social media? If you can see a pattern where you can stop doing something and then set aside writing time instead, even to the tune of 30 minutes, then watch out world.

I do writing prompts at our Kingdom Writers Association gatherings, and these writing prompts are only about five minutes. Then we have people share what they wrote. I have heard some powerful storytelling from people that drives me to tears, or my stomach hurts from laughing. I quickly point out to everyone what five minutes of writing can do. It's powerful, and you need to find the time.

CHAPTER 43
CRITIQUE GROUPS

Critique groups

Proverbs 15:31 "Whoever heeds life-giving correction will be at home among the wise."

C RITIQUE GROUP, BETA readers, editors- oh my! What is a critique group? This is a small group of writers who read a small part of each other's work each week and give feedback to the person. You get feedback for your writing, and you also give feedback to other's writings. It's a beautiful process to go through, and it is also hard. We need to get feedback for our work before we present it to the world. I spent over two years working my first two books through critique from others. It was fantastic to have my work rip to shreds in a good way as I needed solid feedback to make my work even better. It turned my passive voice to an active voice, my run-on sentences were caught time and again, my poorly formed sentences stuck out like a sore thumb, my story content was challenged and ultimately sharpened.

Beta readers are a group of people that you give your manuscript to, so they can read through it and give you feedback. This is when you have completed your book, and you have re-written it to the best of your ability. You need beta readers to give you fresh feedback so you can do one final pass at making it better before handing it off to your editor. Find people you trust and ask them to write notes and give you storyline feedback. Grammar is fine, but you are truly looking for any holes in your story from your beta readers. You need to know if your hero is good and your villain is bad. Do your characters make sense as they interact with one another and do they add to the story or diminish it? I typically print out copies to those who say yes and give them a deadline to return it back to you. I encourage them to write on the hard copy that I give to them as their notes will come back to me. I also like to have an overall synopsis from them where I find out what characters they liked the most or least, was the storyline compelling and gripping, etc

The *final* final stage is hiring your editor. You have done all you can do for your book. It is time for the final step. Hire an editor. This will be your biggest cost as a self-published author. If you land a contract with a publisher, they will most likely have their own editing team to go through it. Once it is edited, don't go back through and re-write things without working through it with your editor. Otherwise, you undermine what you paid for. Now, you still need to go through the final edited copy because you can still find little errors or misspellings. It happens, believe me. It takes a team to get a book out. "It takes a village to raise a child."

CHAPTER 44
DISPOSSESS

J ESUS DOESN'T CAST out the demon named Legion but instead "dispossesses" them. The men were not emptied but instead filled by Christ so much so that the demon's had no space to occupy them any longer. It is not just taking back something, but actually occupying the place where it was. You don't push something aside but instead, consume or inherit that which it formerly was.

It is an incredible word.

In the exhaustive concordance, a defining word jumps out at me, and that is *enjoy*. The word *Dispossess* relates to *enjoy*. Enjoy means to take delight or pleasure in, but it also means possess and benefit from. There is an 'enjoyment' with Christ inside of us. We are his possession and in that there is enjoyment. An antonym of *enjoy* is *lack*, so with our enjoyment we have no fear of lack. Christ is all-sufficient for us, and his indwelling makes no room for anything but enjoyment.

Why do I bring this simple word up in this devotional?

I want to show the depth of words that are out there.

Dig deeper into the meanings of words, and you will discover a rich new level of writing. As an author, I gain more authority as I explore the depths of these words. With them, I can write a sentence that can breathe life into someone reading it.

Action: Study Strong's definition of *dispossess*, which is below for your convenience. Now find a word that you like and do a google search of the biblical definition and see what comes up. Compare that definition with other traditional definitions as well. Ask the Holy Spirit to guide you into His truth about that word. Lastly, have fun exploring as words take on new meanings for you each time you journey to understand them. You will no longer take a word at face value.

Strong's Hebrew

3423. yarash -- to take possession of, inherit, **dispossess**

... yarash or yaresh. 3424 . to take possession of, inherit, **dispossess**. Transliteration:

yarash or yaresh Phonetic Spelling: (yaw-rash') Short Definition: possess ...

Strong's Exhaustive Concordance

cast out, consume, destroy, disinherit, dispossess, driving out, enjoy, expel,

Or yaresh {yaw-raysh'}; a primitive root; to occupy (by driving out previous tenants, and possessing in their place); by implication, to seize, to rob, to inherit; also to expel, to impoverish, to ruin -- cast out, consume, destroy, disinherit, dispossess, drive(-ing) out, **enjoy**, expel, X without fail, (give to, leave for) inherit(-ance, -or) + magistrate, be (make) poor, come to poverty, (give to, make to) possess, get (have) in (take) possession, seize upon, succeed, X utterly.

CHAPTER 45
EVERY MAN IS LOST

"Every man is lost. They just decide whether they are lost in this world or in Him." – Brae Wyckoff

GOD FINDS THE lost to only have them be lost in Him. It is statements like this that create a poetic-mad-crazy-firestorm within me. We wander this world feeling lost and afraid, but when we turn to Jesus, we wander in Him.

There is an amazing quote by St. Jerome, "The Scriptures are shallow enough for a babe to come and drink without fear of drowning and deep enough for theologians to swim in without ever touching the bottom."

This shows me how approachable our God is. It also shows me there is no end to His depth. When I think back to when I was an atheist living my own life, I remember how I was bored with this world in so many respects. I was lost within myself, and my 'self' was a coffin. God gave me life, and yet I chose to live on my own. I just continued to exist inside my skin with no purpose, and no idea of who He created me to be. Thank you, Jesus, for being so patient and chasing after me.

When I finally heard him call my name, I didn't walk or stroll. I RAN out of that grave.

In this life, we either take hold of who we are or hold on to what we were. Let's get totally and insanely lost in Him. We can't reach the bottom as St. Jerome theorizes, but we can sure try. It is in the trying, in the journey, where we find much more than the end of the adventure.

Action: Plan a journey with the Lord. Pray and ask God to show you where He wants to take you. It could be across the world, or it could be down the street in your neighborhood. Enjoy the process, the journey, of going through the planning and execution of your journey with God. I know that He will be speaking to you as a writer and show you things that eventually will be in your book or whatever writing piece you are called to write. Now, this trip could be next month, or it could be next year. You might not have the money but don't think about that. Plan as if you do have the money! Why? Because whatever God shows you and directs you towards, He will provide what you need at the right time. This is a faith journey, and it is scary, but the payoff is God is with you. And He won't leave you. It is time for you to be lost in Him.

CHAPTER 46
DEPRESSION IS REAL

"If your destiny remains buried, then it becomes a 'haunting'; a weighty substance upon you that can turn into depression."- Brae Wyckoff

DEPRESSION IS REAL.

I think we have all fought it in some shape or form, while others have been overtaken by it. I truly believe that inside each person is a longing, a pull from the depths of our soul, to something more. We claw to discover what that 'more' is. We dream about it. We think about it. We dwell on it. All the while, we are quiet, and without a voice because we don't know how exactly to put into words what we feel to those around us. When we can't formulate what that calling is to others, we can run the risk of slowly closing off to it. Life brings nails and eventually a hammer to seal us inside ourselves, never to come out.

Once that happens, our destiny is sealed within this coffin, and we watch it slowly be lowered into the ground. We literally have a funeral service within our heart. We think our calling was never meant to be, that it was a fairytale, that it was for someone else.

While our destiny is buried in this coffin within us, we are haunted by it as we go through life. Something will trigger us during our life's journey that will stir our fate. It begins to knock, then bang, and then loudly thump inside our coffin.

Our destiny becomes a haunting over us, and the weight of it brings us into depression.

But God is the one who resurrects. He is the only one who can bring life back to our calling. And He does it through *us*. We can be the ones He co-labors with. He can partner with us to bring the Shovel of Hope unburying the coffin. And together, God will help us use the Pry Bar of Faith to pop the nails free from the lid. Nothing is impossible with God! And our God is in the business of resurrecting the dead back to life.

CHAPTER 47
WHO ARE YOU?

"Know who you are before you help others. Learn who you are as you help others."- Brae Wyckoff

W E NEED TO understand who we are in Christ. You are a son/daughter of God, and knowledge of this truth should trump everything else around you. Get firmly grounded in the fact that you were called before time, before you were conceived in the womb. You cannot fail unless you choose not to step into who you are in Christ, and even then, you are STILL forever His. God had made up His mind when He called your name, and you answered the call. Few answered, but you did.

As you understand the ramifications of the incredible reality, then and only then can you truly help others to step into their calling. The reality is simple but powerful--that you carry God inside of you, that He resides within you, that you carry the Kingdom of God wherever you step, We will continually be learning and growing in Christ--FOREVER.

The lie is that we can understand all truth in this world. The only truth we need to understand is this: God loves us, sent His son, Jesus, to die for us, Jesus was raised back to life, and those who believe in Jesus are saved. From there, the world opens up for us to help others. When we start helping others, God teaches us more about Himself. In effect, we can learn who we are in Him at a deeper level when we help others.

It is crazy how much growth I've experienced in helping others more than hearing a sermon or reading the next greatest book. Missions trips are a fantastic way to accelerate your growth. The more we walk with God, not just in our consciousness, but physically walk with Him, the more we learn about who we are. He is your Father God and cherishes all the moments He spends with you, even when you're helping others. Perhaps it's especially when you're helping others. He is a good God, and He wants the best for you.

Action: Write about the time (or times) you helped someone through something. But as you write, explore with God the reasons for helping them. What was your agenda for doing so? Go deep with God to uproot any issues of pride that you might not be aware of. Go after the best in you by diving deep into your motives and asking tough questions of yourself to get to the truth. Then release the pride, and ask the Lord to help you as you write, to overwrite your agenda and seal it with His.

CHAPTER 48
HIDDEN TREASURE

"There is treasure in every mountain."- Avery, age 5

THERE IS TREASURE in every mountain.

There is treasure in every person.

My grandson Avery once drew a picture of four mountains. He was around five at the time. He showed the picture to me and proceeded to tell me that it was a treasure map. I looked it over and gave him 'well done' affirmations, but then I realized something was missing. I asked him, "If this is a treasure map where is the "X" that marks the spot so we can find the treasure?"

He looked at me, contemplating what I said, then took the picture back and walked to the table without a word. A few seconds went by, and he came back to me. I reviewed the picture, and I saw an "X" on every mountain. He said, "Grandpa, here is the treasure. It is in every mountain."

At that very moment, the Holy Spirit showed me instantly the meaning behind my grandson's words.

God has gifted each of us, and we need to understand that. Sometimes it takes a lot of digging to find that treasure while, at other times, the gold is right there in front of us. We also need to understand everyone's treasure is different. The saying, "one man's trash is another's treasure," is so appropriate here.

1 Thessalonians 5:11 says, "Therefore encourage one another and build one another up…"

There is power in encouragement. So much so, I believe encouragement is the excavator needed to dig up the treasure that lies within people. Encouragement will stir something within that may have become dormant. I'm not talking about a "good job" or "well done" encouraging word. Instead, I'm referring to a God-sized encouragement where you call out their destiny.

This can come forth as a prophetic word, a word of knowledge, or a word of encouragement, all of which come from God. You become a conduit to express His love for that person. Remember, we are ambassadors of Christ. We represent the King and the Kingdom. All of our encouragement ultimately and emphatically points back to Jesus and gives that person an opportunity to choose Christ.

As Kingdom Writers, we absolutely need encouragement.

Kingdom Writing needs a different mentality from worldly writers. With Kingdom Writers, God orchestrates relationships and people to come into our lives and take us to the next level. You need to be ever watchful for who He places within your path as a writer. Nothing is coincidence, but you also need to be wise and discerning. Be in constant prayer. Encourage those around you and watch what happens.

Change out the word "treasure" to "story" in the chapter phrase. There is a "story" in every mountain. Those called to write require encouragement, the excavator, to dig deep to unearth the storyteller within. You can be the excavator that unlocks the next bestseller inside someone. JRR Tolkien credits his friend CS Lewis for encouraging him to write and publish his little tale about Hobbits

Well, we all know what happened from that encouragement.

Action: As you pursue your career as a Kingdom Writer, don't overlook those that God places around you. Ask the Lord to reveal your encouragers to you. Or, if you have them (and know who they are), ask the Lord to bless them mightily.

CHAPTER 49
FINAL THOUGHTS

Writing is NOT a HOBBY and nor should it be for those called to God's scribal army. Writing isn't just a passion for us but something we have to do. God doesn't want you just writing, but He also wants you to be part of a community of writers. Relationship is so much more important than the assignment, and God doesn't give us the assignment without building the relationships.

TOLKIEN SAID OF Lewis, *"He was for long my only audience. Only from him did I ever get the idea that my 'stuff' could be more than a hobby."*

There is a word coined by the Inklings—*Resonator.*

A Resonator is someone who aligns with someone's work as a writer. They don't placate or make them feel good but instead pushes individuals works to be the best they can be. The Resonator champions the people God has brought around him. He helps others through discipleship, mentoring, encouraging, equipping, and seeing that person succeed. A Resonator does not seek reward or acknowledgment for himself but instead imparts all his knowledge and skills freely to those around him.

Would *The Lord of the Rings, The Chronicles of Narnia, Mere Christianity, The Screwtape Letters* ever exist, were it not for the relationship these men had and the encouragement they gave one another in The Inklings?

CS Lewis struggled with discouragement, anxiety, fear, and doubt. His first desire was to write poetry, but rejection shook his confidence. Discouragement hit Lewis trying to publish his first book along with battling health issues. The Inklings, consisting of over a dozen men, gathered weekly and lifted each other up. If it wasn't for those gatherings, I believe we would not have the books they produced today. Now, if that is true, how many amazing stories lay in the grave today because the writer had no group to gather with, no resonator, no encouragement? How many were, instead, swallowed up by the world?

Don't be swallowed up.

Look for a group to be involved with. Start your own group gathering. Get around others who want to write. Be the resonator they are looking for. You will be encouraged as you encourage others.

One of the names that God has is Breakthrough. He is the God of breakthrough. There are more people alive today than in all of history. We need breakthrough more so than ever.

King David learned about iron and fashioning items with iron from his enemies. He then used this knowledge in making weapons to defeat these very enemies. What the enemy of today controls in publishing and writing will come to its knees when we take our place as Kingdom Writers.

God is calling us to be present and show up to our calling. God wants us to occupy our destiny. He wants us to own it, not rent or lease it, or worse yet, wish and hope for it.

Breakthrough doesn't just miraculously happen. Our breakthrough is planned by God. He has set our breakthrough firmly in place, and we need to step into it. Let your passion drive you there. Everything you have been through in life has prepared you for your breakthrough. God didn't cause the darkness you traversed, but He surely uses it to bring you into your destiny.

One of our KWA(Kingdom Writers Association) members, Rhonda, came up to me and said, "I feel like I caught up to my destiny." Wow, how profound. That statement rocked me.

Some of us catch up to our destiny when we are young and others when we are much further along in our careers of life. Then there are others that never get there, and the graveyard of destinies is added to once again.

At some point in our lives, we must take a stand. We must say enough is enough with the drudgery of life and cry out to God, "I want my destiny!"

I called out to God many times, but the most significant time was the end of 2010. "God, help me to write this book that is inside of me. I need to get it out. Help me. I can't do this without you."

I heard His voice, "Okay, we will write it in 2011."

That set the course of my destiny. I finally caught up to it. It wasn't that He didn't hear my former prayers or that He was ignoring me, it was that He had a specific timeline for me and I found it. His ways are truly not our ways. Remember that. Enjoy the adventure with Him.

We did write that first book in 2011. The Orb of Truth was a labor of twenty years, and it was published in 2012. That was my first victory. Little did I know that I was being prepared to where I am today. Little did I know that I would be teaching thousands of other writers to tell wonderful, creative, life-changing stories to the world.

I think it is time for you to get your first victory. You need a win. Don't get caught up with fame and fortune. Get caught up with God. Get caught up with your destiny.

Apply what you have learned through this book. Apply what the Holy Spirit has imparted to you from this book and from your entire life.

I'm praying for you and your victory as a Kingdom Writer. I want to see the fullness of God working through you to reach thousands, millions, of lives. I'm praying for more Gatekeepers within cities around the world to step into teaching and equipping other Kingdom Scribes. A Gatekeeper is someone that is championing their city and the writers within it. They pray for their city. They pray for Christian writers that are isolated and alone. Gatekeepers end up becoming the answer to prayer from other writers. You will hear others often say, "I was praying for a group like this. I was praying for someone like you to show up in my life."

I hope and pray this book encourages you for years to come. I pray the Holy Spirit invades your heart and mind to write stories you could have never imagined on your own but most importantly I pray you find a group of "resonators" where you write with joy every day of your life.

Kingdom Writers, may the HOLY FORCE be with you!

I would love to hear from you about what you've learned, released, experienced. Send in your testimonies by going to www.BraeWyckoff.com or www.KingdomWritersAssociation.com.

Please leave a review on Amazon and Barnes & Noble. Reviews help others make a decision to buy, but most importantly, your encouraging words matter to us as authors. It is fuel for us to continue to write and to bless others.

If you want to join Kingdom Writers Association, then visit our website at www.KingdomWritersAssociation.com. We have monthly gatherings, workshops, conferences, advances (aka retreats), and more. We have members from all over the world who join our online community along with hundreds of people who are part of KWA here in San Diego, CA.

God bless you!

BIBLIOGRAPHY AND PERMISSIONS

Chapter 2: I Will Send You Scribes

Forums online have suggested- 1,000 to 5,000 books published on Amazon per day

Chapter 3: Imitate Me

Bible sells 50 books per minute

http://weeklyworldnews.com/headlines/49070/top-7-bible-facts/

6 billion copies and counting

https://thebibleanswer.org/bibles-sold-each-year/

Chapter 15: #1 Bestseller

Full Bible translated over 500 languages

New Testament over 2800 languages

Wikipedia information: https://en.wikipedia.org/wiki/Bible_translations

Music- 1 million songs released each year (googled information found in forums)

China building theaters 10 a day

https://youtu.be/Y6cLAJkVkAY

Woodlawn Keynote: This Is Our Time

600,000 to 1M books published each year (google searches will lead you to this information in many forums)

Bowker released that in 2017, 1 million self-published books were published.

http://www.bowker.com/news/2018/New-Record-More-than-1-Million-Books-Self-Published-in-2017.html

Wikipedia info about authors/books- top selling

https://en.wikipedia.org/wiki/List_of_best-selling_books

Broadway - San Diego plays

https://www.sandiego.org/articles/theater/broadway-bound.aspx

Chapter 22: Addison's Walk

Permission granted by CS Lewis Foundation

LETTER TO ARTHUR GREEVES by CS lewis © copyright CS Lewis Pte Ltd.

Chapter 38: The Hero and the Christian

The Hero's Journey by Joseph Campbell- The Hero With A Thousand Faces

Chapter 49: Final Thoughts

Bandersnatch book- Resonators- Inklings

Bandersnatch by Diana Pavlac Glyer and published by The Kent State University Press / Black Squirrel Books (December 8, 2015)

Chapter 49: Final Thoughts

Quote from Tolkien to Lewis taken from Inklings & Influences blog

http://www.cslewis.org/blog/inklings-influences/

"He was for long my only audience. Only from him did I ever get the idea that my 'stuff' could be more than a hobby."

About the Author

Brae Wyckoff is an award-winning and internationally acclaimed author, born and raised in San Diego, CA. He has been married to his beautiful wife, Jill, since 1993, and they have three children and six wonderful grandchildren.

Brae currently travels the world with his wife, training and equipping people in the ways of Jesus Christ, and has ministered to thousands, both locally and abroad. He is the founder of the international ministry called The Greater News (TGN) where he reports on supernatural miracles happening around the world.

Brae is currently the Director of Kingdom Writers Association based in San Diego where he is working with writers of all levels to encourage and empower them to pursue their calling as authors. Brae hosts monthly writers' gatherings with published and unpublished writers to strengthen and spur them on in their passion for writing. KWA has an annual conference called Kingdom Creativity Conference where we have had notable keynote speakers such as William Paul Young, author of the Shack, Lynn Vincent, NY Times Bestseller of Heaven Is For Real, Peter Berkos, Academy Award Winner, and more.

Brae is also the Executive Pastor at Awakening International Church in San Diego. Following in the footsteps of CS Lewis, an atheist turned Christian, Brae has been ministering in multiple capacities within the church body along with scribing several books ranging from non-fiction to fiction. He has won several awards, been an Amazon bestseller, and was a top-ten finalist for the Author Academy Awards. In 2013, he won Best Author of the Year by End of the Universe organization.

Brae Wyckoff takes teams to Israel and Oxford. If you are interested in joining one of these trips then contact him at braewyckoff@gmail.com.

Brae Wyckoff's other books:

Children's Books for ages 2 and up
The Unfriendly Dragon
(Voted #1 Best Kids Book Ever)- Disney artist, Seth Weinberg
The Mountain of Gold
(praised by many educational teachers)

Young Adult Epic Fantasy Series (Amazon bestseller series)
The Orb of Truth: Book #1 of the Horn King Series
The Dragon God: Book #2
The Vampire King: Book #3

Historical Fiction
Demons & Thieves
(won the Readers' Favorite Award)

All titles are available on Amazon and Barnes & Noble
Most titles are in all formats of ebook, paperback,
hardback, and audible.com

www.BraeWyckoff.com